The Final Warrior

Tales of War and Peace

Short Stories and Poetry

by Richard A.M. Dixon

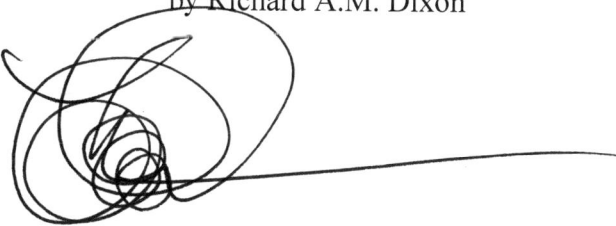

Also by Richard A.M. Dixon

My Heroes Have Always Been Dogs, 2008
(by Richard A.M. Dixon aka Richard A. Dixon)

Dillon's War, The Weretiger of Kontum
Two Harbors Press, 2010

Angels In My Foxhole, Plicata Press, 2013

Dillon's War, Revenge of the Weretiger
Create Space, 2015

Dillon's War, Weretiger's Deliverence
Create Space, 2015

The Tiger of Dien Bien Phu
Merriam press, 2016

Inuit, Create Space, 2016

The Final Warrior

Tales of War and Peace

Short Stories and Poetry

by Richard A.M. Dixon

Table of Contents

PART I: War

INTRODUCTION………………………………………page 6
The Final Warrior…………………………………………..8
An American Hero…………………………………..............22
First Jump……………………………………......…..............38
Valley of the Shadow…………………….....................46
Tiger…………………………………………………....65
A Soldier's Dream………………………………….....…81
Angel……………………………………………….............82
Mission Iditarod………………………………......…91
Finland on Skis……………………….....…………104
Encounter………………………………………113
Night Visitor………………………………………120
Gauntlet……………………………………….....128
30An Old Soldier's Prayer……………………......…134

PART II: Peace

Aunt Marion's Outhouse………………………….page 135
Justice……………………………………….....…138
Boy Scout Jamboree……………………………............146
Jack…………………………………………….153
Tahoma Challenge………………………………164
Greywolf Encounter……………………………176
Search for Gold……………………………......………179

4

The Ballad of Suzie and Sammie.................page 180

The Bummer..188

Sasquatch..203

Alaska Steel..208

Dream of Flight...216

Walkers..218

The Falcon and the Bullfrog.........................228

The Closet of My Yesterdays 235

The Time Machine 236

INTRODUCTION

The tales in this collection of short stories are loosely adapted from my life experiences. Some such as *First Jump* and *Mission Iditarod* reflect autobiographical data from my own life experiences. Names, places, and events are reported as factual as memory permits. Other stories, like *Sasquatch* and *Walkers*, may be tied to facts, but with my imagination acting as an additive.
This book is divided into two parts.

Part I: War takes place during the more than twenty years I spent in military service, not counting my eight years in Reserve Officers' Training Corps: four years in high school, followed by four years at college level. I learned as an Airborne Infantry combat leader and commander in the Regular Army, that a soldier does only two things. He is either fighting a war or training to fight a war. Hence, some of my non-combat activities are covered under Part I.

Part II: Peace contains stories from my youth and the years after active duty when, while still enjoying the benefits of a retired Lieutenant Colonel, I faced civilian challenges.

Writing these stories over the past few years was a restorative experience. I hope you enjoy reading them as much as I enjoy telling them.

Lakebay, Washington: 2016

The Final Warrior
Tales of War and Peace
Short Stories and Poetry
by Richard A.M. Dixon

PART I: WAR

The Final Warrior

My mates and I dropped off the back of an Army deuce-and-a-half and began our ordeal. We were let off at quarter-mile intervals, like roe dropped from the belly of a pregnant salmon, along the single road that partially circumscribes Iriomote, the southernmost island of the Ryukuan chain. The largest of those islands is Okinawa, our home base. We came here for jungle training in preparation for deployment to Vietnam.

Seen from the horizon, Iriomote resembles the back of a dragon, breaching the surface of the sea. At either side of the mountain peak that forms its backbone, the island supports a turtle shell shaped surface of thick jungle. The island is completely surrounded by coral reefs and shallow lagoons. It is altogether a gloomy sight. The soldiers called it, "Eerie-Remote."

As our landing craft approached the island, I studied its contours. *It reminds me of the beginning scenes from the movie King Kong. I wonder,* I thought with more than a little trepidation, *if some great ape waits among the crags in the escarpment looming ahead.* I fingered my M-14 rifle ruefully. *We'll only be using blank ammunition during our training.* Studying the escarpment with some foreboding, I had no idea of the grand adventure awaiting me among its steeps.

We were told the island was uninhabited, saving a few farmers along the coast. It is rumored that they are the remnants of Japanese forces abandoned on the island when it was bypassed for the invasion of Okinawa in 1945. We were instructed to avoid contact with the natives.

The truck slowed a bit. The sergeant signaled me to jump off the tail-gate. I stumbled and nearly sprawled as my feet hit the dirt. I sought cover in the thick vegetation bordering the single-track road.

I squatted in the brush, listening to the sound of the truck fade in the distance. Having experienced this training during Ranger School at Fort Benning, Georgia, I knew what a real hell I faced if captured by the aggressor. *Evade capture at all cost. Resist at risk of actual physical injury. No games!*

I hid and took stock of my tools. *Let's see. Here's a length of string, a camouflage stick, a plastic bottle of joy juice. This mosquito repellant will be useful for starting a fire. Here's my compass, hooked to my combat harness. Both my canteens are full of water. Combat knives, and first aid kit, check. Matches – where are my matches? Ah, here they are, safely wrapped in wax.*

My skin was wet with sweat. The jungle air felt like a damp sponge. I touched up my face and hands with the camouflage-stick. I heard a jeep in the distance and didn't move. I knew the drill. The "enemy" will check the road to see if any of us held back. They will capture any stragglers that appear and cart them off to a POW camp for fun and games. The fun will all be theirs and the games won't be fun for us.

I squatted in the brush, sweating and waiting for the jeep to pass. I took a compass reading and moved south toward the mountain ridge and friendly lines. I picked my way through the jungle vegetation, wanting to put as much terrain as possible behind me. We were taught to move mostly at night and to hide in thick brush during daylight. The aggressors would take advantage of this to snatch up any soldier who took cover too close to the road.

The dense forest hindered forward progress. At times, I was forced to use my fighting knife to cut brush, like a machete. Mosquitoes gathered about me in dense clouds. Rather than use the repellant, the odor of which could be detected for some distance, I periodically applied more of the camouflage stick. It also repelled insects and had no odor. *It's getting dark. Good. Better moving in the dark and less chance of being spotted. There's a clearing ahead.*

Breaking out of thick brush at the edge of a cleared field, I stopped and looked about in the fading light. *There's a native hut several hundred yards away. No people visible, but I'll assume I'm being observed and stay hidden. Those three water buffalos have got me in their sights. Arrayed in vee formation, heads low, facing me and silently chewing their cud.*

Looking to the right I saw that the end of the field was about a hundred yards away. I backed into the jungle, and when I was sure that I could move without detection, began to circumvent the field.

I took a compass reading when I was certain that my course had cleared the end of the cultivated land. I corrected course some fifteen degrees and began, once again to work my way through the brush.

It grew dark. It was so dark, I could barely see my hand when I held it up, feeling my way every step. *I felt sorry for those poor soldiers who hadn't the advantage of Ranger Training. Some of them, I know, will seek capture rather than face this dark unknown.* Taking compass readings more often, to keep myself oriented toward the south, there was some small comfort to be had in the florescent glow of the compass face.

I took a swig of tepid canteen water. It tasted of aluminum. Wiping the sweat from my face, I applied a little joy-juice.

Soon I entered an area where there was a high arboreal canopy formed by tall trees. Their crowns kept the light from reaching the ground, impeding the growth of underbrush. The going got easier. Occasionally I would bark a shin against the knee of a root protruding from the ground.

Filtered light from the stars showed through the tree branches and I found the going a little easier. Stopping to rest at the foot of a monstrous banyan tree, I sank to my butt and relaxed against the cool, smooth trunk, quickly drifting off to sleep.

The land became steeper. I hurried upward to what I believed was the crest of the island. I'd lost too much time sleeping

The jungle canopy ended abruptly at timberline and opened onto a vast expanse that led to the summit. I continued to climb, feeling refreshed by a cool breeze on my back and shoulders. The going was much easier now, despite the steepness of the ascent.

It'll soon be daylight. I gotta find a place to hide where I can't be spotted by the helicopter that's sure to be looking for us. There's something ahead. A hole. Not a foxhole. Too big, but definitely man-made. Big enough for a mortar position. Oh, what a nice cool breeze.

Sliding down into the hole in the emerging dawn, I discovered a flat, well trampled floor that gave out on a breath-taking view of the Pacific Ocean. The Oceanside view of the rounded depression consisted of a well-worn parapet about four feet high. Many people had leaned against the dirt wall until it was worn smooth as if observers had watched the sea for what reason I couldn't immediately fathom. Then it hit me. *Of course, you dumb shit! This is a Japanese observation post left over from the war.*

As I stood mesmerized by the beauty of the sea and the idea that Japanese soldiers had stood where I stood now, enjoying this view, I noticed a pair of binoculars resting on the parapet near at hand. I scooped them up and looked through them to discover they were in good working order. I estimated they were 7X50 power. The lenses were reasonably clean and it looked like the glasses had been used recently. I had an easily 180 degree view of the Pacific Ocean. I stopped thinking about what this all meant and enjoyed the view as the sun rose behind me. It was breathtakingly beautiful. I gazed at this panorama, imagining that I could see the American coast just beyond the end of my vision.

I reclined against the inner wall of what had proven to be an observation post and fell into a deep sleep. Awakening in the late afternoon I was ravenously hungry, but couldn't take the time to hunt for something to eat. Watching the sun set into the Pacific, I felt a twinge of homesickness, and then turned to pick up my gear and move out.

I realized I wasn't alone. Perched on the rim of the depression, I saw a vision from hell. Squatting on the parapet, rising as I turned in the gathering darkness, was an old man with a long wispy beard. He was dressed in tatters, his worn out clothing barely clutching his bone-thin sinews. He had no shoes. He must have been watching the sunset along with me. His eyes were barely visible among the wrinkles. His mouth opened under a white Fu Man Chu mustache to show a nearly full set of white teeth. He screamed a single word; "Banzai!" while he raised both his arms brandishing a long evil-looking saber. With that he leapt straight at me, swinging the finely polished blade vertically at my head. I dodged and swung my elbow into his midriff as he plunged forward and down. Easily I pushed his body aside. With a wraith-like movement he was up and gone over the sea-side of the parapet, leaving me blinking, breathing hard and wondering if I had seen him at all.

I squatted and drew my knife, waiting to face another assault. In the dark now I listened to the night sounds of the jungle surrounding me. I was beginning to think I had imagined the attack when I felt a sticky wetness beyond the sweat running into my eyes. Moving a hand to my brow, I discovered a saber cut to my scalp, not serious, but bleeding profusely as scalp wounds do. I was certain then that I was not hallucinating. I took out my Government Issue compress and covered the wound, wrapping the tails of the bandage around my head.

I stood still, trying to fathom what had just happened. *That confirms it. This was a Japanese observation post left over from the war. This island was bypassed for the attack on Okinawa. Could the old man be a Japanese soldier, marooned by his comrades for twenty years? If that were true, he'd have to be fifty or sixty years old. Can it be possible? Imagine what he must be thinking. He's thinking I'm the enemy and he wants to kill me!*

It was time to move out. I needed to be at the rally point by daybreak the next morning to complete the course successfully. Torn between my need to go and my curiosity about the occupant of this position, I wondered if I could communicate with him. The extent of my Japanese was, *"Hey, GI! You numba ten!"* That wouldn't get me very far. As if in answer to my unspoken question, an eerie voice, somewhere close in the dark, spoke, "American sordier, you die!" More a statement than a threat, the voice was punctuated by the whistle of the saber cutting through air. It seemed that the sounds came from the direction I needed to go, but I wasn't sure.

Twice I changed direction plunging forward. Twice I was turned back by the threatening whoosh of the saber. I was held prisoner in the bunker. I hunkered down, waiting for my assailant to mount another attack. The night advanced into the early morning hours. *This is ridiculous.*

I'm held at bay by a remnant of the Imperial Japanese Army, an army that doesn't exist anymore—By a man old enough to be my father, maybe my grandfather. It's a macabre joke. By noon tomorrow they'll have choppers out looking for me. I just need to hold out. Wait! I've got it. I'll surrender! Surely he understands what a white flag means. He'll take me prisoner. Then the choppers will come and police both of us up. Let's see. What can I use for a white flag? The only white thing I have is my under shorts. Oh well, they'll have to do. Mom would not like this.

I dropped my baggy field trousers, and slipping them down over my jungle boots, I stepped out of my skivvies. Stooping to pick up my trousers, I felt something sticky on my leg. Looking down, by the dim light of a waning moon, I saw a dark lump on the inside of my thigh. There, looking like an extension of my scrotum was a humongous leach all bloated by its gorging on my femoral blood. Sickened by this gruesome sight, I willed myself not to tear it from my body.

Wait! Wait! Wait! You do that and you'll leave its head in your leg to fester. What to do. What to do. Oh yeah. I remember from the Boy Scouts. Place a match stick to its body immediately after dousing the flame and the heat will make it release its hold. Okay. Okay. Match. Here we are. A cigarette would be better.

Clutching my matches unsteadily I tore one away from the mass of wax coating. I drew my knife and rubbed the head of the match against its serrated handle. Immediately the match ignited. At the same time I heard, "AIEEEE!" followed by screamed Japanese words. These I could not fathom, but I expected to be attacked momentarily. My

15

human foe would have to wait while I dealt with this slimy horror that had attached itself to me.

What a sight I must be, standing naked from the waist down, pants around my ankles, a burning match in my hand. I would have laughed out loud save for the horror I felt at the sight of that gorged blood-sucking slug romancing my scrotum.

The match had burned down and was burning my fingers. I blew it out and pressed it against the leech near what I thought must be its head. Nothing happened. In a moment I heard a sound like water in a wet log, placed on a fire, screaming as the heat dries it. Then the leach withdrew into itself and fell to the ground. I saw my own blood squirt out from under my boot as I crushed the bastard to death.

As dawn advanced, I was once again taken by the beauty of the Pacific vista. I rigged my skivvies on a stick and waited for my erstwhile enemy to show himself. I didn't wait long. With a scream of some unintelligible Japanese, he hopped nimbly onto the parapet, saber held high.

Only now did I recognize the blade as a katana. I had seen replicas of its sort in shops on Okinawa.

I waved my white flag and offered my best Warner Brothers Production bow in the old man's direction.

Smiling, showing those sparkling teeth, he hopped down off the parapet and strutted toward me. Holding the saber to his side he advanced toward me looking like a character from *The Bridge Over the River Kwai*. I backed cautiously to the opposite side of the pit. The old man stopped at its center. Looking at me disdainfully, he barked an order and pointed at a place in the pit. I moved to the spot and sat down. He seemed upset that I displayed no fear of him. The truth was it was all I could do to break out laughing at the picture we made.

He moved to the sea side of the pit, and slid his katana into its ragged scabbard. Everything about him was ragged and old except his blade. It alone remained shining and fresh. Now, spreading his arms to the sea, he spoke. He jabbed at various loci in the water. Then, finished with his rhetoric, he looked questioningly at me.

I started to rise, shrugging my shoulders because I understood nothing of what he wanted.

"Ieh!" He shouted, drawing his katana again and spread his legs menacingly. Half standing I froze in place, spreading my hands and shaking my head to signify my failure to understand.

Impatiently he reiterated his words, this time with more gesturing with his razor-sharp blade in one hand. I began to understand. I said, "No, Chief, I did not come from anywhere in the Pacific." I pointed toward the ocean and shook my head vigorously. "I came from Okinawa." Shifting from right to left hand I pointed toward the opposite side of the island toward the South China Sea and my home base.

There was silence as my captor looked at me with wide eyes and open mouth. "Ieh! Okinjiwah ieh!" He looked at the ground and shook his head. "Okinjiwah . . . ieh . . . Ieh!" He looked at me. I understood—he was pleading with me to tell him that I had not come from Okinawa.

I nodded and grasped my hands before me. "Yes. I came from Okinawa." I knew what this meant to him. He seemed to shrink before me. Gone was the proud warrior

17

with the Don Quixote attitude. He was replaced by a decrepit old man. His hands trembled.

After a while he seemed to gather himself. He said something to me in Japanese, and turning his back to me for the first time, led me out of the pit and a short way down a well-beaten path to a grass hut. We entered and from a corner my host gathered up a radio and hand-crank generator. These he set before me and commanded me by gesture and voice to crank the generator. I remembered seeing this type of hand generated radio in a movie somewhere. I knelt and began cranking. He gathered up the hand-set and began a liturgy. "Moshi, moshi, ano ne?" He spoke again and again into the mouthpiece.

When he was convinced that no one would answer his calls to his long-vanished headquarters, the old soldier set the handset down and, without looking at me, moved to a hearth in another corner of the hut, and began to blow on the ashes. Soon he had a fire going and placed an earthen pot on the flames. Then he moved to a cabinet fashioned from bamboo and removed from it a small cloth bag. Standing before me, he motioned me to kneel by a small table. Kneeling opposite from me he opened the bag and poured some dried leaves into his hand. "O cha. Ichi ban." he said to me and I understood that he was about to brew the last of his tea.

Without rising, he moved on his knees from table to hearth, and prepared the tea. Rising he went to his cabinet and from it took two small cups and saucers. With some small ceremony, he placed the cracked china on the table. Soon the smell of tea began to permeate the hut. Lifting the pot from the hearth, the old soldier knelt and poured the hot amber liquid into our cups. During the last of his movements he began talking or chanting. When these tasks were finished, he took up his cup, nodded to me to take up mine, and said, "Gomen' nasai." Then he bowed his head and was silent.

I never tasted a better tea. Its aroma permeated the hut. I looked at the old warrior, his eyes averted.

In silence we drank our tea. Then the soldier gathered himself up and drew his katana from its scabbard. Holding it by the blade, both hands forward, he offered it to me and said, "Domo arygato gazaimas." I accepted the weapon as he bowed deeply. He said more words that I couldn't understand, but one caught my attention. He looked into my eyes and said, ". . . seppuku." At the same time he drew his fist across his midriff.

I understood that he intended to die and that he wanted me to kill him. I looked away. Shaking my head vigorously, I said, "No! No, I cannot do this." I looked into his eyes again. It was as if I could see the beaten soul of an entire nation in them. Here was the last of a proud generation of warriors.

The old man did not speak again. Rising and walking to a sleeping mat, he lay down and closed his eyes.

I sat on the floor and wondered what to do. *Technically he is my prisoner now. According to the Geneva Convention I am responsible for him. But that's for handling of prisoners of war. How does it apply here?*

The whup-whup of an approaching Huey helicopter interrupted my ruminations. The old man opened his eyes and looked at me. His eyes held a question. I rose and tried to explain to him with gestures that it was an American helicopter, probably searching for me.

I ran to the pit and waved my makeshift white banner, but it was too late. The Chopper had already passed. Its drone faded rapidly. I dropped my flag and returned to the hut to find my prisoner slumped as if he had tried to rise and failed. I stooped and grasped him by the shoulders. His head lolled and I moved my arm to support it. He appeared to be dead. I checked for a pulse and found none. His spirit had been relieved of its arduous earthly duty.

I lifted him and placed him gently, respectfully on his mat. Sitting on the floor beside him I pondered what to do now. I felt honored that I had known a soldier so steadfast in his duties that he had remained alert all these years. *Old man you were an authentic hero; the last warrior of a vanishing breed. If I take you back with me they may not understand. They may treat you like any other indigenous corpse. I can't allow that.*

All night I kept a vigil by his side. When morning came I knew what I had to do. I gathered brush and branches and built a funereal pyre suitable for a military hero. Placing the old warrior's stiffened body on the top of the pyre; I gently positioned the katana on his chest. Then I went to gather suitable tinder to get a fire going quickly.

I sat down to wait. After a while I heard the sound of the helicopter approaching. I rose, ignited a match, and touched it to the tinder. Immediately it flamed up. Running to the pit, I waited for a sighting of the chopper. Looking toward the hut I saw that the flames were building nicely. The straw roof had caught and was throwing off a grand plume of smoke.

The chopper flew over my position. I waved my white flag. I thought they saw neither the smoke nor me. Then they circled back and I knew that rescue was imminent.

As a cable was lowered toward the pit, I looked back to see that the hut was totally enveloped in flames. I was assured my unknown soldier had received a warrior's funeral. I leaned against the bulkhead, Pratt and Whitney engine vibrating against my shoulders, and composed a story about how I had become disoriented and wandered around in the jungle for two days.

An American Hero

When the Vietnam War came to an end in 1972, there were some 2,000 military dogs serving in South Vietnam. Some were trained as guard dogs, serving on American facilities and supply dumps. Others were trained as scouts and worked in the jungles, on point for our soldiers, alerting them to booby traps and ambushes. Many were killed in action. The dogs that had survived when the fighting was finished were turned over to the Army Quartermaster Corps for disposal. They were all euthanized in theater.

Recently, military service dogs completing their service were awarded full status as retired military veterans. Now they are rehabilitated to civilian life and adopted out.

This is the story of Little Joe, a canine hero who was killed in action at the Battle of the Ia Drang Valley in the central highlands of Vietnam near the Laotian border. The year was 1965. Little Joe, the canine protagonist of my story, was born on Okinawa and never set foot on American soil. He was whelped in 1964 to a litter of Japanese bred German Shepherds and destined for security duty of American dependents living on Okinawa.

While this story has been embellished somewhat for the sake of drama, the facts are true to the best of my knowledge. The characters, human and canine, are real.

When I was assigned to the 173d Airborne Brigade on Okinawa, in February 1964, my first job was to find housing for my young family of four. The family would be allowed to join me when I made arrangements for their housing. Though I didn't know it at the time we were soon to be six.

During a tour of the island trouble spots, conducted by the Military Police, I was told by my guide, " If you're looking for housing in the civilian community you better get a dog, the bigger and meaner the better."

"Why do I need a dog?" I asked.

"We got gangs of Okinawan 'Stealie Boys' who can slip into your house and steal the rings off your fingers without ever waking you up. They can't get to the military housing because it's all gated and guarded."

The next day I was given directions to the house of one of our officers, a colonel, who had just been allocated on-post housing and would be moving in a few days. I immediately went to look at it. The house wasn't much, one-story cinder block, but the location, in Awase Meadows, on a ridge descending between two cane fields, overlooked the Pacific Ocean among palm trees and sugar cane. *I'd never be able to afford a place with a view like this, stateside.*

The colonel's wife (I can't remember their names), smiled and shook my hand as she let me in to look at the house.

"Welcome to Okinawa. Do you have children?"

"Yes, I have a girl, Cindy, who will be entering the first grade and a toddler Evelyn who is almost terrible two."

"Your wife will like this location. The Army school bus comes by just at the foot of the ridge."

As I stepped into the house I noticed a large dog standing in the middle of the room, looking intently at me.

23

"Oh, this is Rufus. He guards the place—thinks he owns it. He won't bother you, but don't try to pet him. He's not very friendly toward strangers."

I hadn't owned a dog since I was a boy. This big fellow looked like a junk yard dog.

As the colonel's wife showed me through the house, chattering about island and family life in general on Okinawa, the dog followed, making no sound. When we finished the tour she said, "Would you like a glass of iced tea? I've just made some fresh."

"Yes thank you. That would be nice."

As we sat at the kitchen table she continued.

"It gets very warm here in the afternoons, but there is always a breeze from off the ocean. Do you like the house?"

"Oh yes, ma'am. It'll do fine. The MPs told me I should have a dog. I guess that's true."

I nodded my head toward Rufus who watched us as he lay on the kitchen floor.

"Yes, Stealie Boys are particularly common on this side of the island. They haven't bothered us. Rufus gets the credit for that. Do you have a dog, Lieutenant?"

I shook my head.

"Lieutenant Wargo's German Shepherd recently had a litter. I'll call his wife and see if they have any pups left."

She picked up the phone and after a short discussion said, "Oh good I'll send him right over." Then she hung up.

"Sheila Wargo says they have just one pup left, a male. If you're interested, you should go over there right away. Their pups are registered Japanese Kennel Club. Hard to come by."

I stood holding the small black ball of fur cupped in my hands. I lifted him close to my face for inspection; he looked at me with eyes like shiny black buttons. *This must surely be the runt of the litter. He can't weigh more than a couple of pounds. This is the dog that's going to protect my family from thievery?"* As I studied him, he studied me. Then deciding something, he licked my nose. The softness of his touch melted my heart. *Hey, I'm supposed to be a big bad-ass Airborne Ranger. You found me out didn't you? Just a softie at heart.* I held him close to my chest.

"I'll take him. Guess I'll call him Little Joe."

The dog showed his approval of my choice by peeing on my shirt.

"Can you take care of him until I get my new quarters squared away and my family on the island?"

"Of course. We've all been in your shoes. Just let us know when you want to pick up Little Joe."

She smiled and handed me a towel.

I wrote a check for the dog.

"Oh, he's so cute," Brenda took the puppy from me. She was pregnant with what was to be the sixth member of my growing family, Christopher Brian Dixon.

"Better get a paper towel," I said.

"I see why you named him Little Joe, but, look at those feet." She took one paw in her hand. "He's not going to be "little" much longer.

That night, Cindy, my six year old said, "Daddy can Little Joe sleep with me? Please?"

"No, Sweetheart. Joe is supposed to be guarding us. He has to stay on the floor where he can get to the papers Mommy laid out. He's not house-broken yet."

Later, that night after we gone to bed, I heard Little Joe moving about. I thought, *good. He's beginning to patrol the house.* I dropped off to sleep, only to be awakened by the dog's crying.

"He misses his mother," Brenda said.

I lay there in the dark, awake now and thinking, *so what?*

When I woke again it was to the alarm ringing at 0500. Time to get up. I shut off the alarm and reached over to Brenda and tell her it was time to make coffee. As I touched her, I felt a lick on my arm. I sat up and turned the light on. There was Little Joe asleep between us. Some watch dog.

It took about three days of watching him and moving him to the newspapers before he was housebroken. In a week, he had grown about five pounds and was beginning to take charge of security. He began to sleep on the floor under the head of our bed. Several times during the night he would wake me with his padding through the house checking on each of the kids as they slept.

There was one drawback to his sleeping under the head of the bed. He farted often and silently. Brenda would sit up suddenly in bed and exclaim, "Oh God!"

I was a rifle platoon leader. I needed my sleep.

At five months Joe was all legs and ears as he began to take charge of the children. Chris had been born and Joe spent a lot of time guarding his crib in a bedroom next to ours and at the side of the house. In the tropical climate of Okinawa we always kept the windows open and covered with screens.

I came home from work one day to this tale from Brenda.

"I was changing the baby today when an Okinawan man came to the door. The first I knew of his presence was when Little Joe growled. It was the first time I heard him growl. I went to the front room and saw a man standing outside the screen door. He had a basket of something. He took something out of the basket and held it up. I couldn't tell what it was and I didn't feel safe moving closer to see it. The man said, 'Okesan, you buy?'

"I shook my head and said 'ieh.'

"He said more loudly, 'Okesan, you buy!' This time it was more of a demand than a question.

"'No!' I said sharply. 'You go now!'

"The dog stood in the front room, his head down, his teeth showing. He was growling lowly.

"Then the man grabbed the door handle and shook it, demanding once more that I buy whatever it was that he was selling. At that movement Joe jumped up and ran at the man barking loudly. The man beat a hasty retreat down the hill. Joe hit the screen and I thought he was going to go right through it."

Brenda was telling me this as I sat in a bamboo rocker enjoying a martini she had mixed for me. Little Joe sat in front of me, looking at me with intelligent eyes, tongue lolling. I was certain he understood what Brenda was saying. I studied him. He had grown quite a bit. He appeared awkward, but this look was deceptive. The dog was fast and very agile.

"Joe, you're a hero. You protected the family. I won't have to worry about them when I'm gone off-island."

Our unit spent a lot of time training in far flung places like Korea and Taiwan. I hugged Joe tightly around his thickening neck. He gave me a great sloppy kiss with his long tongue. This was a tongue that could pick up an egg dropped on the floor with a single lick.

One day, as the girls were playing outside with some neighborhood children, Joe nipped one of them in the course of playing. Rules on the island pertaining to dogs were: first bite – ten days lockup. Second bite—death.

No exceptions.

Brenda called me at work and told me what had happened. I called the vet and was told I'd have to turn Joe in for ten days detention in the kennel. I went home to get the dog. As I put his leash on, he looked sadly at me. He was trying to tell me that he was sorry.

"I'm so sorry, too. Joe, but I gotta take you to doggie jail, my buddy."

The second day Joe was in the slammer, we were hit by a Steelie Boy. The only thing that aborted the attempt was that he tried to get in the window over Chris's crib. He woke the baby who let out a howl. Brenda got up and turned on the kitchen light. Then she went in to see what the matter was. I woke as she returned to bed.

"Huh . . . wuzzup?"

"Nothing I thought the baby needed changing. Guess he was dreaming . . . or something. Go back to sleep."

Next afternoon when I returned home from my unit, Brenda said, "Come with me. I want to show you something."

I followed her into the baby's bedroom where she pointed to the screen behind the crib. It had been damaged. A large L-shaped cut told me a Steelie-Boy had been thwarted in his attempt to rob us, by the baby's crying.

"Looks like they know Little Joe's not here, I said. "We have to sleep with one eye open for a few days 'til he comes home."

I visited the Army kennel every day to see Joe. Every day he'd cry and scratch at the bars on his cage, trying to get to me. I wanted to hug him, but they wouldn't let me open the cell. Each time, when I left Joe, he howled like a banshee.

The day I brought Joe home from the kennel, we had a big party. Joe weighed eighty pounds and was growing fast. I barbecued steaks and gave Joe a whole T-bone which he devoured bone and all, in less time that it takes to tell about it. The kids played with him. We took Chris, who was crawling now, out of his crib and let him play on the living room floor with the girls and Little Joe. The dog was absolutely gentle despite Chris' sticking his fingers in Joe's eyes and pulling his fur.

I walked him around the outside of the house, letting him get a good smell of the ground outside the baby's window. That night the Stealie-Boy struck again. I guessed he hadn't got the word.

This time he tried to enter our bedroom window. The first I knew there was something amiss was when the dog launched himself across our bed and, with a blood-curdling snarl, thrust himself through the window and onto the dark form that was crouched in our window frame. Joe took him down, screen and all.

Later Brenda and I talked about how it must have felt to have eighty pounds of German Shepherd suddenly in his arms as he fell to the ground.

I looked out the window into the dark. I couldn't see anything, but the screams and barking were coming from the direction of the cane fields in the gully behind our house. I threw on my pants and boots, grabbed a flashlight, and ran outside. I prayed the dog had not been made a victim of the thief's knife.

Brenda stayed inside the house, seeing to the children and turning all the lights on.

All had gone silent in the gully. I shined my light around looking for signs of anything. I could see multiple trails broken in the cane.

"Little Joe. Are you there, Joe?"

I saw movement as the dog dashed up and out of the gully. Approaching me at the edge of the lawn, I could see streaks of blood on Joe's chest. I feared the worst. He bounded happily up to me, and as I knelt to inspect him for wounds, he licked my face joyfully. Daylight was coming fast. Finding no wounds on Joe, I feared that there might be a body down in the cane field.

During my Okinawa in-briefing, I remembered the MPs telling our group that if we happened to kill an Okinawan criminal outside in the act of attempting to burglarize our house, the best thing to do would be to drag the body into the house and place a knife in his hand before calling the military police. I was prepared to do just that.

As dawn broke, Joe and I descended into the cane field. I carried my combat knife for protection, should we encounter a bad guy. The cane was disturbed and trampled in several places and I found several large spots of blood.

How could one man bleed so much and still walk away from it?

I kept close watch on the dog, but he didn't alert to anything. I went back to the house after searching the cane field, relieved that I didn't find a corpse lying in the grass.

Over breakfast, after I took a shower with Joe, Brenda asked, "Shouldn't we inform the police about this attack?"

"I was thinking about that while I was searching the cane. What if the police consider this incident number two for Joe?"

"Oh dear God! I never thought of that. We better hope the neighbors didn't see anything."

"We better just keep our mouths shut. Brief the children."

Nothing ever came of that incident and shortly afterward we moved into quarters in the army garrison in the Sukiran area just behind the island headquarters. While Little Joe's service was no longer necessary, he retained his position as guardian of the family.

He had grown up that night in the cane field.

On May fifth, 1965 our brigade was deployed to South Vietnam. Initially we were considered on temporary status for ninety days. Our mission was to defend Bien Hoa airfield, freeing up the Army of the Republic of Vietnam troops for offensive operations against the Viet Cong.

After ninety days our status was made permanent. We were committed for the duration of hostilities.

A twelve month rotation policy was established some months later.

Soon thereafter that it was announced that our dependents would have to go stateside. Our commanding officer, Brigadier General Williamson, announced an arrangement with the Air Force to rotate each soldier with family on island, back to Okinawa by C-130. We were each authorized four days to help our families prepare for transport to the U.S.

When my turn came, I eagerly boarded the Hercules transport and headed for home. We arrived at Kadena Air Base in the early evening. I caught an Okinawa taxi, called a Skoshi Cab for the Sukiran area where I lived.

The cab dropped me off at the gate. They were not allowed in the American housing area. Walking up the hill with my duffle on my shoulder, I suddenly became aware of the quiet. I stopped and looked around.

There wasn't a sound. In just a few short weeks I had forgotten what the absence of the sound of war was like. I looked up the block toward home and tried to see which of the lights were mine. Suddenly I saw a dark form moving swiftly toward me. He ran under a streetlight and I thought, *What if this isn't Little Joe?* Instinctively I reached for my weapon. Then realized I was unarmed, just as Little Joe leapt into my arms.

I dropped my duffle and sank to one knee. He licked my face and cried like the pup he had been a few short months ago. He must have weighed over a hundred ponds now. He had recognized my coming long before I'd seen him.

"Joe. Little Joe, you've grown up. How I've missed you, boy."

The dog began to cry. We cried together as I hugged him close. He licked my face furiously. Together, we walked up the street toward home.

"Joe. Joe where are you?" I heard Brenda calling him. I could see her standing in the door.

"We're here, Honey," I said.

I heard her gasp. Then, pushing the screen open, she ran to my arms as Little Joe danced around us. I was home.

As I walked into the house Cindy came running.

"Daddy, Daddy,"

Evelyn ran into the room. I was surprised to hear her talking.

"Daddy, Daddy,"

Chris, walking now, stood by the door, thumb in his mouth, wondering what was going on. He didn't recognize me. I scooped him up and reminded him who his father was.

We spent the evening playing on the floor. Little Joe lay sprawled on the floor letting the children crawl over him.

I was home.

The four days passed by too swiftly. Brenda and I spent more time just being together than preparing for the move.

Before I knew it, it was time to go back to the war. I hugged each of the children. Then I hugged and kissed Brenda, trying to capture the scent of her to carry with me in the hard days ahead.

Lastly, I hugged Little Joe tightly. I searched his eyes trying to tell him how much I counted on his taking care of the family.

I didn't know this was the last time I would ever hold him.

A day later I was back in the jungle, counting the days by combat patrols, ambushes, and heliborne assaults.

I made captain and was moved to battalion headquarters. I was low dog on the promotion list and found myself number twenty on the waiting list for three company command slots. When the chance came to transfer to the First Cavalry Division, just entering the war, I took it, hoping to get a command in that unit.

During this time one of the daily letters written by Brenda and received by me intermittently, brought bad news. She was back stateside and wrote to tell me she had not been able to handle the kids and Little Joe too, during the move. When the Army had asked for volunteers in the K9 corps, she volunteered Little Joe.

She was heartbroken, but didn't know what else to do. I grieved, but understood. She had three small children to care for and was headed for where she didn't know. We had no home and no parents to look to for help. I had told her to go to Fort Benning, Georgia. I believed that would be my next assignment.

I prayed that Little Joe would serve honorably.

When a company commander was wounded and shipped, out I got my chance, and in December, 1965 found myself leading a rifle company in a blocking position against the Cambodian border. The 7th Cavalry had punched a hole in a hornets' nest on the opposite side of the Chu Pong Mountains and now I found myself with my rifle company at the far end of the Ia Drang Valley, determined to stop several thousand North Vietnamese (NVA) with two hundred soldiers.

Shades of George Armstrong Custer.

We held our positions, expecting the worst, hoping for the best. We were in a perimeter defense surrounding a battery of 105 mm howitzers firing missions around the clock in general support of the division. Word was they were firing mostly in support of the 7th Cavalry who were getting creamed on the other side of the mountain.

It was quiet except for the occasional NVA who was caught trying to infiltrate to Cambodia. We were shipping them out as we captured them, to division headquarters for processing as POWs.

I learned that another rifle company from my 8th Cavalry was coming in to land in my firebase, pass through, and begin a sweep toward the Ia Drang Mountains. I watched as the slicks began to land and drop their infantry, like so many tadpoles, onto the ground.

One ship dropped off a dog handler and his black German shepherd.

I sucked in my breath. My heart skipped a beat.

I ran toward the dog. It was, it had to be Little Joe. He had filled out and walked as proudly as any soldier.

I slowed as I approached dog and handler. I knew that if it really was Little Joe and I interfered with the handler, the dog might break training and no longer be suitable for service.

I stopped short. The men in my company watched me closely, thinking perhaps I'd gone section eight. The dog handler came toward me. I stared at the dog.

The dog looked at me. As we locked eyes, I knew it was Little Joe. He started to react. The handler, feeling the dog's hesitation, pulled on his leash and spoke to the dog.

"C'mon Blackie, we got work."

As the rifle company moved off and into the mountains, the handler and his dog led the way. I watched them go and felt proud of my Little Joe.

He was truly an American hero.

Later when I had finished the mission and returned to base camp, I tried to discover what happened to Little Joe's unit.

I read in one of the 8th Cavalry unit logs that a scout dog named "Blackie" had been killed in action on the west side of the Chu Pong Mountain summit during the battle of the Ia Drang Valley.

The log goes on to say he was shot while trying to save his handler from enemy fire.

This brief entry in a unit log served as his epitaph, until now. His body was probably left on the battlefield for the ants.

I have written this story to remind us all of the canine heroes that served and still serve our country, some never lived here.

Little Joe's picture hangs on my wall. Our family will always remember him as a true American hero.

First Jump

"Six minutes!"

The Jumpmaster sounds off and gives hand signals, ensuring that he is both seen and heard, over the noise of the twin C-119 engines, by the forty soldiers about to make their first parachute drop.

Six minutes, I think. *My four years ROTC training and three weeks of 82d Airborne Division ground training have come down to this. Six minutes to go before I jump out of a perfectly good airplane and hope my parachute opens before I hit the ground.*

Honor graduate in 1961 of my ROTC class at the University of Washington, in Seattle, I am offered a regular commission in my branch of choice, selection of my first duty assignment, and an entry date any time within twelve months of graduating. I decide to take advantage of the full year to pay off my student loans. After several months of working at Boeing, I am itching to get it on with the 82d Airborne Division, my selected assignment. I volunteer for duty commencing on Friday, September 15th.

Reporting for duty under a test program that places a cadet at his first duty station for up to a year before attending his Basic Officer Course, I sign in at Fort Bragg, North Carolina. At Division Headquarters, where I report in khaki uniform with tie, I am told to report to the Adjutant of the 2d Airborne Battle Group, 501st Regimental Headquarters. From there I am to be further assigned to Company B.

I walk into the Company B orderly room where I confront the First Sergeant. I say, "First Sergeant, I am Lieutenant Dixon, reporting for duty."

"Ah . . . right, Sir," he looks me over carefully. "I'll tell the CO you're here."

The sergeant disappears into an inner office and reappears a minute or two later. "Captain Hyatt will see you now." He points the way into the Captain's office.

This is a big moment for me; reporting to my very first commanding officer. I want to make a good impression. I step smartly to the front of his desk and snap a salute. "Sir, Lieutenant Richard A. Dixon reports for duty."

Captain Hyatt returns my salute and says, "I have no use for a leg lieutenant. You are dismissed."

Confused, I make my way back to the battle group headquarters and again face the Adjutant, "Sir, Captain Hyatt says he has no use for a leg."

"Well then, Lieutenant, I guess we'd better get you enrolled in jump school as quickly as we can."

The Adjutant makes a telephone call.

"You'll report to the Jump School at 0600 on Monday morning. The Sergeant Major will give you directions. Good luck, Lieutenant."

On the following Monday, four days into my Army career, I begin a three week course of instruction in what is one of the tougher training regimens in the Army.

All the intensive ground training I've gone through; dawn 'til dark physical conditioning supplemented by specialized training in how to jump and land safely have not prepared me for the noise and the rush of adrenaline as they open the doors in preparation for our first parachute jump.

I look around me, studying the faces of the other troopers. I am the lead jumper in the starboard stick of twenty soldiers. Across from me is another stick of twenty. Their eyes tell me they share my sense of impending danger.

Adding to the intense heat inside the aircraft, each of us is entombed in our parachute harness. We are sweating profusely.

My right hand moves automatically to the D-ring on my reserve parachute, strapped to my harness at belly level. I am reassured by its cool aluminum presence. The lines of an airborne cadence ditty run through my mind, "Stand up, hook up, shuffle to the door. Jump right out and count to four. If that chute don't open wide, I got another one by my side."

The plane bounces around, buffeted by pockets of Carolina air, heating rapidly under September sun.

Two troopers vomit, made sick by the heat and the motion of the aircraft. Gorge rises in my throat from the stink of the vomit. I fight down my own feeling of nausea.

"Get ready!" the jumpmaster shouts and signals. I wonder at his ability to make himself understood in the cacophony of noise made by the engines and the airframe as it is jerked around, buffeted by the wind.

Now the Jumpmaster, standing in the back of the aircraft, and extending both arms forcefully toward the troops, commands, "Stand up!"

We work our way onto our feet in the bouncing airplane. Our T-10 Parachutes are suddenly heavy on our backs. We stand facing inward. We've practiced this drill countless times in mock-ups on the ground. I watch my fellow soldiers closely to see if they are as nervous as I am. Along with the excitement I can taste fear. We are collectively afraid, not of dying, but of failure. *What if I freeze at the last minute?*

"Hook up!" shouts the Jumpmaster.

We clip our static lines to the thick cable that runs the length of aircraft and yank on them to shut the slides. Then we thread the locking pins through the slides to lock them shut.

As the C119 descends to the 1200 feet jump altitude, it begins to bounce more violently in the hot air. Each trooper stands, holding onto his static line, like an umbilical cord connecting himself to the belly of this great whale of an aircraft. We are attempting to steady ourselves against the behemoth-like skin of the fuselage. Beads of sweat cover our faces. By now, our dominant collective motivation is, *let me out of this airplane!*

"Check static lines!"

Each trooper faces aft, and grasping the static line of the man to his front, runs his hand along the line to where it is connected to the chute, making sure it is free of snarls and is properly connected.

"Check equipment!"

Each of us checks the chute of the man to his front to insure that it's properly rigged and that all straps are running free and there are no twists or snarls. We have all been checked by the jumpmaster at least once, before boarding the airplane. This will be our last chance to detect any problems.

"Sound off for equipment check!"

I, and the first few men in each stick, can hear the jumpmaster's command. The assistant Jumpmaster stands toward the front of the aircraft and repeats the commands. Each of them prominently displays the hand signals. The troopers echo the commands, confirming that they have heard or seen, and understand them.

Beginning at the end of each stick, each soldier sounds off, "Number twenty, okay!" and slaps the man in front of him on the butt.

When I hear, "Number two okay!" and feel the slap on my butt, I signal with my left hand.

"Number one okay!"

The Jumpmaster looks forward to see that his assistant has checked number twenty for both sticks. Then he nods.

I look into his eyes and see that he is nervous as we are and is intent on performing his duties perfectly, as I am. My life depends on it.

Now the fuselage is shuddering and bucking as we fight to retain our balance. We continue to stand facing the rear of the aircraft. The Jumpmaster faces us. Tension is building.

The doors open. A fierce wind swoops around us, tugging at us as if coaxing us out into the sky. I look back at the soldiers. Each of them seems intent on what we are about to do. I feel proud that I see no fear in them. They will jump. Our communal adrenaline rush is maxed out. I know that my own eyes are large, not with fear, but with anticipation. We trained hard for three weeks, preparing for this moment.

"Stand in the door!"

I shuffle aft and pivot left to place both hands on the frame of the aircraft door. I look out and down, but have no sense of height. Countless bungi jumps from the thirty-four foot tower have helped remove the fear of height. I feel the slip-stream pulling at my cheeks. Any fear that I might have felt early in my training, is absent now. I am gripped by the excitement of the adventure. I remember that we were instructed to make a vigorous exit so as not to risk entangling with our opposite stick members. I remember to watch the light at the side of the door. It is red. When it turns green, I will jump into the air whether or not I hear the command or feel the slap on my butt.

"Go!"

The command is followed by a solid rap on my butt.

The light is green.

I vault forward into the sky and am immediately gripped by the slipstream of the airplane. I look down, straight back at the tail of the aircraft, because my body has swung upward and outward from the fuselage. It feels like I am being born, spewed forth from the uterus of this aluminum behemoth.

I count, "One-thousand, two-thousand, three-thousand, and four-thousand."

Feeling the pull of the canopy as it opens, I rejoice in the immediate weightlessness and the comparative coolness of the air.

I am momentarily worried. The pull is not nearly as strong as I had felt bunji jumping from the tower. I grasp my risers and look up to see that beautiful olive-drab canopy deployed above me. I Look up at the departing planes. I see the ship disgorging paratroopers like a guppy birthing its young.

I look to see any signs of white, the telltale signal that means trouble and someone has had to deploy his reserve chute. There is no white to be seen.

I float, weightless toward the ground. It is gloriously quiet as I drop, slowly undulating, back to the surface of the earth. What a peaceful feeling it is.

It lasts all of one minute. I am aware of the earth approaching rapidly.

Our drop zone, called Sicily DZ, is the largest and sandiest drop zone at Fort Bragg. I sink to my ankles in soft sand and tumble like a beached flounder as my chute deflates around me.

Hallelujah! I'm alive!

And so alive do I feel as I jump up and begin to roll my chute. I stuff it into my kit bag and join the others for the short trek to the assembly area, I am thinking, *I am the King of the World! Not thirty days into my military career and already I am a paratrooper. At least I will be after four more jumps. Bring 'em on.*

More than twenty years later, I am making my 300th and final jump on this same drop zone before I retire from active service. The thrill has been the same as I felt on that first jump. Now as I move toward the assembly area where I am to stand for my retirement ceremony, my body is heavy with the subsiding of the adrenaline rush. I have been privileged to face danger with these brave comrades.

Valley of the Shadow

We moved out in single file into the perpetual gloom of the deep jungle. Our battalion of 850 men had made its first helicopter assault into "War Zone D," an area controlled by the communists a few clicks north of Saigon, South Vietnam. Anything that moved in the zone was presumed to be enemy. Our Brigade of 3500 men was to conduct Search and Destroy Operations in the Viet Cong's back yard. So far we'd had no enemy contact. The jungle was strangely quiet after the departure of the noisy Huey slicks.

Our orders were to use what daylight remained to move out as swiftly as possible from the landing zone, and then to form platoon-sized circular defensive perimeters for the night. Our Alpha Company, 2d Airborne Battalion, had its three rifle platoons, comprised of forty-seven men each, deployed two forward and one back in reserve. All three were moving in single file, one man behind another. The vegetation was so thick the troops were required to maintain less than fifteen feet separation in order to maintain visual contact.

My second platoon was forward and to the right. To my left was Lieutenant Snookie Wrangel's first platoon. Bringing up our rear was third platoon with Company Headquarters. Also trailing were our two 81mm mortar squads. The battalion was arrayed similarly. To our left was Charlie Company. Bravo Company trailed in battalion reserve. Thus we were arrayed for battle in threes modeled historically on Napoleonic battle formations, by battalions of about 800 infantry soldiers, companies of about 200, and platoons of 47 bad-ass paratroopers. Our brigade, a force of nearly five thousand could cover close to twenty square miles and do battle on any front, including our rear. For once, we had plenty of artillery support. A full battery of six 105mm howitzers (towed) was placed in direct support of our operation. Forward artillery observers (FO) were placed with each company of infantry.

My platoon was on the right flank of the battalion. The left flank, some miles away, was screened by the battalion reconnaissance platoon led by my good friend, Lieutenant Roger Haygood.

We moved out cautiously, first squad leading, point man out in front, barely visible from my position just behind the first squad leader, Sergeant Gurley. Directly behind me was my radio-telephone operator (RTO), Specialist Fourth Class Walker.

We hadn't moved a hundred yards when I signaled the lead squad to halt. Each man knelt in the brush: point focused straight ahead, next man facing left, next man facing right, and so on alternating down the line.

Sergeant Gurley turned to me, waiting for instructions. Leaning closely I said, "We're making too much noise. Pass the word for each man to check the man to his front for rattling equipment and tape it up. My RTO has to change to his short antenna. The long one keeps hanging up in the brush." I tapped Walker. "As soon as you can, call Company and tell them we're held up to re-wrap equipment."

"Roger."

When each squad leader signaled "ready," we moved out. The point made his way cautiously through the trackless jungle, stopping at every suspicious point, alert to the presence of trip wires and booby traps.

"CO says to speed it up," said Walker.

I nodded. When I was certain that all noisy equipment was wrapped in tape, I pumped my fist upward twice to signal the platoon to move out smartly. Tapping Sergeant Gurley I said, "We've got to keep the pace as fast as possible to keep up with the rest of the company."

Gurley nodded and moved up to his point man, telling him ostensibly to speed it up, but not so fast as to get careless.

We moved through the jungle quickly, but cautiously, alert to any movement to our front or to our flanks. The continued silence was eerie. Even the insects seemed muted.

We moved along for thirty minutes or so. I was watching the point man closely. Private Franklin was a screw-up in garrison; always getting into trouble with the MPs. He'd been busted from sergeant several times on Okinawa, but in the jungle he had the instinct of a cat. I depended on him to keep us from walking into an ambush, or tripping a booby trap.

As I watched him work and thought of what he could have done with his career, I saw him freeze. He held up his left hand. The other riflemen crouched in their designated ready positions. Sergeant Gurley moved forward. I crouched, holding my hand up, signaling all my squad leaders to watch me for further guidance.

Gurley returned with the news that Franklin faced a rice paddy.

I signaled the other squad leaders to remain in position. Then turning to Walker, I said, "Tell Company we've found a rice paddy. Request instructions."

"Roger." Walker made the call and listened.

"Sir, the old man says to stay put. He's on his way up."

I nodded and signaled for my squad leaders to come to my position. My second squad leader, Sergeant Tracy was the first to join me, followed by the third squad leader, Sergeant Franco, the weapons squad leader, Staff Sergeant Brown, and my platoon sergeant, Sergeant First Class, Reynaldo. I counted on Sergeants Brown and Reynaldo more than the others because they were veterans of the Korean War and were the only soldiers in my platoon with combat experience.

They silently gathered around and squatted in the brush. "We have a rice paddy to our front. I'm going up to take a look," I said. "The old man's on his way to our position. We'll hold what we've got until we get orders. Be ready for anything. Any questions?"

They all gave me the thumbs up and started back to their squads except Sergeant Reynaldo who hung back. He said, "Sir, I don't like it. It's too quiet."

"I know, Top. Stay near the rear of the platoon and make sure everybody stays awake. Be ready for anything."

Sergeant Reynaldo nodded and moved toward the rear. I depended on his experience and battle knowledge. If we had to form a line to attack, I would control the right side of the platoon, Reynaldo would work the left. We'd practiced all our plays, like a football squad, back on Okinawa.

We waited for what seemed a long time. It would soon be dark. Captain French finally arrived accompanied by his RTO, Jones the company medic, and First Sergeant Smith. We moved forward to where we could see the rice paddy.

"Okay, Tom," The captain said to me, "I see two water buffalo toward the far side of the paddies. Looks to be a mile or so distant. You need to keep an eye out there. Do you see that hill directly in the middle of the paddy area?"

We looked at a heavily wooded hill about 500 feet high with a flattened hilltop of about twenty acres.

I nodded and he continued, "I need you to occupy it by nightfall. Think you can do it?"

"Sir, Second Platoon can do anything. I'm a little worried that the paddies may be booby trapped. That will slow us down."

"Nonsense, Charlie had no warning that we were coming. He won't have had time to set out traps. Once you have control of that hill, we can drain the paddies and deprive the VC of the rice. I want you to move out smartly. I'm sending the company medic with you. Do you understand?"

I nodded. Sending Jones with me meant the captain believed I was the most likely to sustain an attack.

Captain French and the company command group moved back to the rear. Momentarily I thought about calling my leaders forward again, but decided they'd understand. I signaled the platoon to move out.

Our platoon formation looked small and vulnerable as it spread out onto the rice paddy. I signaled and signaled again for the platoon to spread out laterally, maintaining maximum distance between each man in the event of incoming fire or booby trap.

We moved knee-deep through the dark water of the paddies in the open. We watched the tree line on the far side of the paddies, knowing that enemy fire would be launched from there.

One hundred yards. We moved cautiously expecting to draw fire at any moment. Two hundred yards. I noticed that the water buffalo had disappeared. Nothing moved except us. It was getting colder with night gathering, but I was sweating. Still no sound, but that of the men moving through water accompanied by the buzz of mosquitoes.

I thought of the Bible verse . . . *yea though I walk through the valley of the shadow of death, I*—automatic weapons opened up on us from farther beyond and to the left of our objective. Rounds began kicking up water all around us.

"Hit it!" I yelled and dropped behind a berm. Coughing and spitting out foul tasting paddy water, I signaled for the two machine gunners to open fire on the far side of the rice fields. Walker moved up and handed me the radio handset.

"Alpha six this is alpha two, I'm receiving fire from one, possibly two Chicom heavy machine guns. Returning fire with my LMGs (light machine guns). Enemy is beyond Rifle range. Request indrect fire support. Over."

"Six here. Give me coordinates."

"Wait, out." I reached in my side pants pocket and pulled out my map. Luckily I had waterproofed it before we launched.

"Six, this is Two, sector four, coordinates 257349, over." Rounds continued to splash all around us. So far no one had been hit. The men were so low in the paddy I was afraid one of them might drown. No telling what sorts of slimy creepy-crawlies might be sharing the mud with us.

"On the way, wait."

I looked along the line. We looked like so many frogs afloat in the water waiting for insects. A mortar round landed short of the tree line, throwing up a cascade of water.

"Add two five, fire for effect," I screamed into the handset. To the men I shouted, "As soon as the friendly rounds start to land, everybody hightail it for the hill. Got it?" the squad leaders and the platoon sergeant all responded with a thumbs-up.

The mortars were right on target now as explosions blossomed along the wood line. As one, the platoon jumped to its feet and ran for the base of the hill. We had about two hundred and fifty yards to cover. "Keep in formation," I shouted as the faster soldiers began to outdistance those who were slower and more heavily weighted down. The enemy fire had stopped as soon as the mortar rounds began to land. The Viet Cong were either laying low or had skedaddled. Either way, my main concern was that they would catch us running in the open.

Reaching the base of the hill, just as night fell, we gathered in a tight perimeter to catch our collective breath, listen and watch in the gathering darkness. A pall enveloped us like a blanket. There were no sounds. No night birds calling. No monkeys chattering. No insects. Nothing. Troopers dropped their drawers searching for leeches they might have attracted in the rice paddies.

We crouched at the base of a lone hill rising some two hundred feet. It was completely surrounded by rice paddies. Hills rose around the paddies creating a pocket that seemed deserted of all life save ourselves.

I whispered, "Pass the word for Sergeant Tracy to report to me."

It was getting really dark, almost pitch black. "Yes, sir," whispered Sergeant Tracy moving in on my position.

"Sarge, I want you to send a couple of your better men forward to recon ahead of us as we move to the crest of this hill. They are to move slowly and watch out for booby traps. We'll wait ten minutes and move the rest of the platoon forward very slowly. We're supposed to have a moon later on tonight. Any questions?"

"No, sir, but I'd like to send a full fire team up so there's immediate response to any trouble."

"Good idea, Sarge. Do it. The platoon will move in fifteen minutes from now."

I squatted at the edge of the woods, trying to get a feel for this night. Looking out over the paddies we had traversed, I could see the stars begin to appear. They were comforting.

"Sir," whispered Walker, "Old man's on the line. Wants a sitrep."

"Six, this is Two. We are at the base of the objective, preparing to move to the crest. We have no casualties, out."

"Who's that?" Movement close by had me reaching for my .45.

"Just me." It was Sergeant Reynaldo.

"What do you make of this quiet, Sarge? It's got the men spooked."

"Seen it before in Korea, just before an attack. Not much happening here though. Can't get my chops around it."

We were silent for a time and then I said, "Look. Through those trees you can see the stars. Makes me feel safe. Whatever happens down here, the stars will always be there."

"Whatever," the sergeant said as he moved away.

"Pass the word," I whispered. "We're moving out. Order of movement two, three, one. Weapons with three. Single file. I'll be with two. We move in one minute." I wondered if the word would become garbled as it passed down the line. Like that crazy parlor game we used to play. The men of the second platoon always seemed to sort it out correctly. We moved out and upward, silently picking our way through the underbrush. We'd been moving for a short time when the word was passed back that the patrol had reached the top with negative contact.

We established a perimeter defense around the crest of the hill. As was our custom, I walked the line to insure the men were digging in deeply and all weapons were placed correctly, while Sergeant Reynaldo set up our command post (CP) and fixed chow for Walker, himself, the medic and me. The moon rose in the night sky, bringing comfort to the troops. I looked out over the rice paddies and saw nothing moving.

"Gosh, that's almost as purdy as a Georgia moon," offered Private First Class Gregory as I knelt behind his foxhole.

"Indeed it is," I said. "I proposed to my wife under just such a Georgia moon."

"Yore wife a Georgia peach?"

"Yes, indeed. They're the best kind." I tapped the top of Gregory's helmet and moved on.

"Kind'a spooky tonight, ain't it Lieutenant?" I stopped by Sergeant Gurley's squad.

"Yes, it surely is. Too quiet. Keep your men alert, Sarge. Have you got your Claymores and trip flares set out"

"That's a roger," he responded.

Returning to my impromptu CP near the crest of the hill I found a hole big enough for four almost finished and Sergeant Reynaldo working his C ration magic.

I sat on the hillside looking up at the moon and remembering the times I shared such a moon with my wife and hoping I would share it with her again. My eyes began to water as I felt the nearness of her. Her hair so soft, her blue eyes reflecting the light of the moon.

"Incoming!" Someone shouted.

I caught myself dreaming of other times and other places. I heard the "whoosh" of the mortar round just before it impacted on our hillside.

Flash! Bang! The projectile landed off down the hill, beyond our position. It was followed by another round closer to the top of the hill. I was glad I'd been so insistent that our men dig in deeply and we'd laid telephone wire between squads.

"Walker, gimme the radio to Company. Get reports from all the squads."

"Alpha Six, this is Two. Objective secured." I continued, "Enemy 82mm mortar registering on our hill. Request H&I (harassing and interdictory) fires vicinity last fire mission, over."

"Alpha Two, this is Six. Roger, hold your position until ordered otherwise. H&I approved. Out."

"Sir, squads report no casualties. All men are dug in deeply. Awaiting instructions," Walker reported.

"Good, What do you think, Top Soldier?" I turned to Sergeant Reynaldo.

"Hard to say, but my gut tells me Sir Charles is preparing to attack our vacation home away from home."

"Walker, get me all the squad leaders on the horn for an orders call."

"Roger."

As 81mm mortar rounds began falling on the far wood line, Walker handed the telephone to me. "All squads up, sir."

"Okay, listen up. Here's the situation. We're in a perimeter defense around the top of this hill. Indications are that the enemy will attack sometime during the night. Probably from the west where we received earlier automatic weapons fire. Our mission is to hold this hill until ordered off.

"Sergeant Brown."

"Brown here."

"Make sure your machine guns have interlocking fire down our Western slope. Your position will be with the northernmost gun. Do your belts contain tracers?"

"Roger."

"Good. Each rifle squad will send out a two-man listening post, fifty yards to the front. Make sure they don't get tangled with the trip wires.

"Sergeant Franco."

"Franco, here, sir."

"Your squad is least likely to face an attack, so you'll be in reserve. Send one man to my CP to act as messenger."

"Roger."

"Are there any questions?"

When there were none, I said, "Good keep this line open. Maintain one hundred percent alert until I say otherwise. Out." I handed the telephone to Walker.

"What culinary delights have we tonight, Top?" Sergeant Reynaldo was known for his ability to make chicken soup out of chicken shit.

"For your enjoyment tonight we have the specialty of-a de house-a, Beenie-Weenies au gratin followed by Spaghettios ala mouse turds. For desert-a we will tickle your taste buds with sausage patties almost-a rotten." This last was punctuated by a volley of enemy mortar fire that landed squarely on our position. We ducked our heads as rocks and dirt caromed off our helmets.

"Aw shit!" said Sergeant Reynaldo. "There go the Spaghettios."

I made out six rounds landing on the hill. Then it was quiet. I grabbed the telephone. "Report!"

"First squad; two rounds landed in my sector. Negative casualties. Out."

"Second squad; one round in my area. No casualties. Listening post reports movement to their front. Someone is throwing rocks at them."

"Did you say rocks?"

"That's the report."

"Okay, everybody stand by." I turned to Sergeant Reynaldo and said, "Top, Second Squad says they're receiving incoming rocks. What do you make of that?"

"Well, sir, if we were in Korea the commies would be using rocks to feel out our positions before attacking. My guess is that we can expect Charlie to hit second squad—and soon."

I picked up my telephone again, "Tracy pull in your listening post. Gurley, you and Franco too. Franco, report."

"One or two rounds hit close. No casualties. Suspected movement to my front."

"Roger, all hands alert!" Turning to Walker I said, "Give me the handset." I called company headquarters.

"Alpha Six this is Alpha Two, over."

"This is Alpha Six, sounds like you've got some action on your hill. What's happening, over."

"We took six mortar rounds. No casualties. My men are well dug in. We've had movement on both sides of our perimeter. I've pulled in my listening posts. Sergeant Reynaldo believes we can expect an enemy attack shortly. I agree. Request artillery plan to provide 360 degree defensive fires on call. Over."

"You got it, Tom. I'm alerting third platoon in case you need reinforcement. Out"

I was sweating. We were receiving our baptism of fire. I could feel it in the air. I fingered my Saint Michael medal and murmured a short prayer. *Saint Michael, patron saint of*

57

paratroopers, watch over us and keep us safe from harm this night.

The moon set bringing a darkness that was oppressive. I labored to breath. Suddenly, rifle fire started up in 2d squad area. I heard one of my machine guns open up on that flank. Almost at the same time I heard AK47 fire on the opposite side of the perimeter. Our entire perimeter opened up.

"This is Tracy. I'm taking a major frontal assault by at least a platoon. Pelky is down. Send medic, Over."

"Medic on the way," I said as I waved two fingers for Jones to move to 2nd Squad's position.

Third squad came on the line. "This is Franco. We've got major fire all across our front. Estimate at least a platoon. We're holding for now."

"Roger," I said. The only squad not engaged was the first, under Sergeant Gurley. "Gurley. Platoon reserve. Be prepared to counter-attack in any direction at my command."

"Roger."

"Alpha Six this is Alpha two. Fire Mission! Execute pre-planned fires all around my perimeter. Over."

"Roger, wait out."

We waited for what would be a full artillery barrage surrounding our position. Above the sound of firing we could hear the whistle of rounds incoming. They impacted almost simultaneously across our entire front. We could see by the momentary blossoming of light that we were surrounded by hundreds of enemy soldiers bent on our destruction.

"Gurley here, I'm taking major fire to my front."

"Roger, keep up the fire."

"Tracey here, I have two casualties. Ammo running low."

"Roger, hang in there."

After minutes that seemed like hours the firing slowed and then stopped. We'd driven Charlie back for now. I called for a situation report before calling the company commander.

"Let's have a sitrep."

"Gurley here, I got one KIA, three WIA, two able to fight. Redistributing ammo. Approximately fifty rounds per man available. Negative contact at this time."

"Tracy here, three KIA, three WIA, ammo at twenty rounds per trooper. We need help to continue."

"Franco here, one KIA, four WIA, one able to continue. Ammo low.

"Brown here, One gunner down, both machine guns operable. Two hundred rounds left."

Then it was quiet. Too quiet. I called for flares. By the white undulating light of artillery flares I could see that we were totally surrounded by several hundred Viet Cong. I reported my problem to company headquarters. I was told to hang in. Now I saw the flash and heard the explosions of grenades landing on both sides. Mortar rounds fired from across the paddies started to land all across the hill. Rifle and machine gun fire was continuous. The enemy was breaking through what barbed wire we'd had time to lay and was about to assault our position. Stories of the Alamo flashed in my mind.

"Alpha Two, this is Alpha Six, over."

"Alpha Two, go." I was beginning to think that we had cashed it in. I didn't want to hear bullshit from the captain.

"This is Six, hear this. We're sending first platoon to relieve you. Hang in for a little while. I'm giving you priority of artillery fires. Out."

"What do you think, Top?"

"I think we bought the farm. Time to say yer prayers, lieutenant."

"I will, sergeant." *Holy Mary, Mother of God be with us in our hour of need. Send your angels. Send my angels. Send any angels . . . if I have guardian angels let them come now!*

I grabbed the telephone hoping the wire hadn't been knocked out. "All squads, if you can hear me, answer up!"

"Gurley here."

"Tracy, yo."

There were a few seconds while we waited for Sergeant Franco to respond for third squad in order. Then Sergeant Brown broke in with, "Brown okay, but only two belts of ammo remaining."

I turned to no one in particular in the dark and shouted above the noise, "Somebody send me that runner from third squad!"

"Mellencamp here sir!" He answered at my shoulder.

"Right!" I grabbed him by the arm. "Monitor my message and run it down to Sergeant Franco. Don't come back."

Picking up the phone again I said, "It's not looking too swuft for the home team. I'm about to bring artillery down on top of us. Pass the word to duck as deeply as you can into your holes. Good luck. Out."

Mellencamp required no further guidance. He was off and running. I hoped he'd make it. "Walker, give me the handset . . . Walker?"

"Walker's hit," Sergeant Reynaldo shouted into my ear. "I'm your RTO now." He handed me the handset.

"Alpha Six, this is Alpha Two, Request all available fires directly on my position. I say again, put everything you've got on this hill ASAP, over."

"It's that bad, Tom?" the captain responded.

"It's that bad, captain. Tell my wife my last thoughts were of her and the kids . . . out."

"Okay, Tom. On the way. Be advised that Wrangel's platoon is moving across the paddies under light resistance. I'm going to hold them up until after . . . after we cease fire on your hill. Good luck. I hope you get to give your own message to your family . . . out."

I squatted down, hugging the dirt in the wall of our CP. I could hear the medic working over Walker. He had been busy moving from position to position helping those he could. He said, "Can somebody give me a hand with this bandage? I can't use my left arm."

I was about to ask him what was wrong when I heard the "whoosh" of incoming rounds followed by the distant reports of the howitzers. In an instant I lost all ability to think as the rounds descended on our position. There was a terrible din, worse than I ever imagined. We were tossed about like rubber dolls as each round impacted. One side of our foxhole collapsed onto Walker and the three of us worked to free him.

We appeared to move jerkily in the flashes of the artillery rounds, like the characters in a silent film.
I imagined myself as Charlie Chaplin.

Just as I was sure this total cacophony would last forever it stopped as suddenly as it began. The darkness was palpable. Then I realized I had my eyes closed. Opening them, I was amazed to see a brilliant light—not the cold phosphorous light of a flare, but a warm light with the brightness of the sun. There was total silence and I thought I must have gone deaf. I looked over at Sergeant Reynaldo and the medic. They both huddled at the bottom of the hole, their faces covered by their arms. Neither of them moved. I stood and looked out over the edge of our CP. The sight was like a hill from home just after the loggers had felled all the timber. But what captured and held my attention was the bright warm light. In its midst, close at hand, yet distant stood a tall figure dressed in white. In his right hand he held a gleaming sword.

"Who . . . who are you?" I tried to say. I couldn't hear my own voice.

"You know who I am." His lips did not move, but I could hear him clearly. His voice was like music. "You wear my pendant around your neck. You invoke my presence every time you jump from an airplane. I heard your cry for help. I am here."

There was no noise or movement of any kind. Only his voice and as he raised his sword, his was the only movement. As I followed his eyes toward the perimeter, I could see clearly to the edge of the world. From the sky appeared six cobra gunships. They seemed to move in slow motion as they spread out and covered my entire perimeter with the high-whining squeal of their Gatling-gun fire. The earth before them was torn apart as well as the communist soldiers in it. They made no sound. Body parts fell like rain on our position.

It all stopped as quickly as it had started. The cobras departed. The bright light dimmed. My heavenly apparition disappeared as quickly as it had appeared. It was dark again. It remained quiet. I took a deep breath. *What happened? Did I really see the archangel?*

"You okay, Lieutenant?" I jumped as I realized that Sergeant Reynaldo stood at my shoulder.

"I'm fine, Top. You okay?"

"Yeah, but I feel funny. Never been under a direct barrage like that. Hope I never will again. Walker's dead. Medic too. I feel like I oughta say a prayer. Thought I was deaf from the shelling, but I hear you okay. What happened to the VC attack?"

"Cobras moved in under flares and wiped 'em out. Better call the squads."

I looked for and found my handset in the dirt at the bottom of our hole. "Hello, anybody there?" I waited a minute then cranked the telephone and said, "Hey, Gurley, Tracey, Franco, Brown. Anybody read?" No answer.

"Guess the lines are all out. I'm going down to see if I can make contact, Top. You try to call the company and tell them to stand by for a sitrep."

"Roger sir."

Moving along the line from position to position I found roughly half of my soldiers still alive, though dazed from the shock of the overhead artillery fire. At each position I warned them that friendlies might be approaching and to challenge before firing. Sergeants Gurley and Franco were KIA. I collected a runner from each squad and returned to my CP.

My Platoon Sergeant greeted me with, "The radio is fucked. How 'bout I rustle up some grub?" he asked in his best Gabby Hayes (an early western movie star) imitation, which wasn't too bad, all things considered.

"Sounds good. We got any coffee?"

"Got plenty of powdered coffee, but not much water. Let me see what these troops you brought with you got on 'em."

We managed to scrounge up enough water for a cup of coffee each and the top sarge saw to it that each soldier got a hot C ration.

We waited for dawn.

At first light, three shots rang out from a single M16 rifle. I sent a runner in the direction of the firing to confirm that we had made contact with the first platoon. After a time, the runner returned with Snookie Wrangel, the first platoon leader.

I jumped up to shake his hand. "Snookie, you bastard, I never thought I'd be glad enough to see you to kiss your boots."

"Now Tom, let's not get all teary-eyed about it. I've moved my men into your positions. Your medic is working with my men to help the wounded and collect the dead. Choppers will soon be here to move us all to base. Man, you've had quite a time of it. Better give the old man a call, then tell me all about it."

He handed me his handset and I called in, "Alpha Six, this is Alpha Two, over."

"This is Alpha Six, I am happy to hear your voice, Tom. I know your situation from Snookie's report. Are you alright?"

"I'm 5X5, sir. Your request for Cobras saved the day."

"I never requested Cobras. They appeared out of nowhere and disappeared as quickly as they came. Thank goodness for your flares or they wouldn't have known where to go."

"Roger, sir. I hear Hueys coming. I better get to work. Out."

"What the hell happened here, Tom?" Lieutenant Wrangel asked.

"You wearin' your Saint Michael medal, Snookie?"

"Sure. You bet. Never jump without it."

"Good. Better keep it handy."

Tiger

I saw him first in a dream. He came to me while I was asleep. In my dream I opened my eyes to see him, staring at me. I gazed deeply into those piercing yellow eyes and was mesmerized by the sight of my own face reflected in the eyes of the tiger.

I blinked. I wasn't looking at a reflection. I was looking at me through the tiger's eyes.

The tiger licked his whiskers and purred.

I tried to move, but was held immobile by his riveting gaze. The tiger crouched, bringing his face closer to mine. His purring morphed into a deep-throated growl. I saw his long ivory fangs and felt his hot breath on my face.

I looked into the bottomless pit that was his maw. I felt myself beginning to fall into that abyss when suddenly . . . .

I felt someone shaking my shoulder. "Wha . . . what's up?" I woke and sat up. I was drenched in my own sweat.

"Sir, sorry to disturb you during siesta, but there's an urgent call from Kontum City. It's the commander, sir."

"Well shit! Why's he calling me this time of the day? He knows I was up all night, flying support for a ground attack!"

Shaking my head to clear lingering visions of the tiger, I said, "Sorry Sergeant. I didn't mean to sound off at you. The Colonel can wait while I wash my face. Tell him I'll be a minute."

"Roger that, Sir." The Sergeant returned to the radio room. I could hear him talking on the radio. I left my canvas cot, and stepped to a basin I kept full of clean water, an indulgence in my world of primitive subsistence.

Drying my face on a dirty G.I. towel, I entered the radio room still in my skivvies, donning only a pair of rubber flip-flops to preserve my vanity.

"Yes, Colonel O'Neil, This is Major Guinness," I said picking up the handset.

"Guinness! We got a situation here. I need to see you ASAP."

"Can I wait for a chopper, or do you want me to drive to town?"

"Aw shit! Stay there. I'll get a chopper and be out in a half hour."

"Roger that. I'll be waiting on the pad."

Static on the line told me the Colonel had hung up. I went into my hootch to dress. *Maybe I should shave? Aw, to hell with it. The boss knows I've been up all night.*

I changed my mind and dug out my shaving gear. Drawing a canteen cup of sun-heated water from the overhead water tank, I looked into my slivered wall mirror, salvaged from wreckage of the Tet offensive.

Shit. You look like you've just seen a ghost—or a tiger.

I scraped at the stubble with a dull blade. I thought about my assignment up country to this beautiful piece of hell called *Kontum*. God created it beautiful. Man made it hell.

The sound of a helicopter setting down on the district pad brought me back to the present. I quickly dried off and hurried to meet the Colonel.

We sat sharing coffee in my team mess hall. The Colonel took a long sip of brew, and then without further preamble said, "We got a problem in Kontum. The American 4th Division troops are complaining that their front lines are being raided by tigers, almost on a nightly basis. Colonel Johnson reports tigers are stalking his fox holes and dragging soldiers out and eating them."

"Whoa. That's not good. Aren't they putting out trip flares and booby traps to detect and destroy marauding animals?"

"It's not as simple as that. There is one tiger that seems to be able to avoid any traps placed by the Americans. The Montagnards are saying that there is a weretiger hunting out there."

"Weretiger?"

"Yes. A supernatural creature that can change its shape to human and back at will. According to the Yards, this tiger cannot be killed by ordinary means. It requires conducting rituals handed down over the ages."

The Colonel pulled a pipe from his shirt pocket and filled it from a tobacco pouch he took from another pocket.

I couldn't believe my ears. I felt like a participant in a Sherlock Holmes episode—The Tigers of the Baskervilles. I shook my head.

"Here's what I want you to do, major. I want you to personally conduct a hunting trip to destroy this tiger.

When you have tracked down and killed the animal, turn it over to the Yards for disposal. Do I make myself clear?"

"Yes, sir. I'll take Phan Trang along as a guide. Knows all the Yard headmen. I've never been sure he's not a VC, so I'll take Jake along as insurance."

"Jake?"

"My dog. He can smell a VC a hundred yards away. If Trang is VC, Jake will smell him out.

"Okay. Just make sure you come back alive, or I'll have your skin."

We both laughed at the Colonel's macabre joke. "You got any whiskey?"

"Now Colonel, you know we don't allow alcohol out here."

"Just checking. Brief me when you have your plan put together, come to my compound in the city. We'll have a scotch or two then."

"Will do, sir." I escorted him to his helicopter.

"Trang, my friend, you know every inch of the terrain in this district. I'm counting on you to lead me to the tiger. Tell me what you will need."

"What weapon you carry, Thiu-ta? (Major)"

"I have an M-14. It's been used as a sniper rifle, so it's fitted with a night-scope. Takes 7.62 ammo and packs plenty of punch."

"Puncha?"

"Enough power to kill a tiger."

Trang smiled, gaps showing where he was missing teeth. He nodded and said, "I will fashion two rounds special ammunition for you."

"Special?"

"Yes, Thiu-Ta. Two rounds 7.62 millimeter bullets, with special Montagnard . . . how you say . . . prayer?"

"Ah, you mean a blessing by your mountain gods?"

"No, not blessing. Blessing is for Christians. This prayer more like curse. Weretiger need special curse for killing." His eyes were expressionless as he looked at me.

I felt a shiver run up and down my spine. Trang smiled again. I looked at Jake who relaxed in his special chair. His ears perked up and he growled in a non-committal way.

Eyes narrowing, Trang looked first at Jake, then at me. "Thiu-ta bring dog?"

"He knows his way about the jungle. He is not coming to hunt the tiger. His job is to protect me from VC."

I looked at Trang. If he got the point he didn't react.

I patted Jake on the head and scratched behind his ears.

"Okay, we leave tomorrow."

In my cot that night I thought about my recurring dream of the tiger. I awoke in the pre-dawn, energized and anxious to hunt.

Trang and I set out early, Jake following close on my heels. We went overland rather than risk spooking the tiger with the noise of a helicopter.

Jake didn't like his trail position behind me. He was used to ranging out ahead, looking for VC. Trang insisted that the dog take up the rear so as not to spook the tiger.

The Montagnard slipped through the brush like an eel among river rocks. We trekked upward into the mountains. Trang stopped, skirted a tree to the right, and continued on. As I came abreast of the tree, I saw it was crawling with stinging red ants. If I brushed against the tree I would be bathed in a shower of thousands of ants, each one with a poisonous bite.

The air this time of year was cool and invigorating, and relatively free of mosquitoes. Reaching the crest of the range, we were bathed in a cool breeze.

We stopped to rest and briefly enjoyed the view across the valley stretching far below. The war seemed distant.

We moved on, downward now, toward the triple canopy jungle that was the home of our "weretiger."

The sun set and it grew dark. At a sign from Trang, we hid in the brush beside a trail. A VC patrol passed by, walking as if they were embarked on a leisurely Sunday stroll. Jake lay beside me, belly to the ground. I could feel a growl building deep within his chest. Wisely, he kept silent.

After the VC were well clear, we picked our way silently through the jungle. Its nightly symphony of sounds grew louder as the night wore on.

Trang led about ten yards to my front. I stayed just close enough keep him visible in the gloom. Jake followed so close behind; I could sometimes feel his nose touching my heels.

Trang stopped, and stooped to investigate something on the ground. I nearly collided with him. My mind had been wandering. As I squatted alongside Trang, he put his finger to my lips in a silent warning to keep quiet. Then he grasped my index finger, placed it on the ground, and traced the outline of a large paw print.

I had never seen a tiger's paw print before, but I knew what it was. It was at least six times larger than Jake's. This was a big tiger. By the feel of the impression, I judged it was made within a day or two at the most.

Trang leaned close to my ear. "This is big tiger. Bigger, I have not seen. We rest here. I must see this track in daylight to believe."

Rain fell as we hunkered down in the dark to rest. Trang kept part of his body over the paw print to protect it from washing away. I squatted under a tree with Jake huddled close to my knee. Sometime during the night I slept. I dreamt again of the tiger. As before, he grew larger and larger in my consciousness until I felt myself about to plummet into the chasm that was his maw.

Trang's hand on my arm startled me. The rain had stopped sometime during the night. Daylight was just breaking. A light, cool breeze carried the scent of unnumbered jungle blooms, hastened by the rain to strut their various scents in an effort to draw pollinators.

We stooped together, studying the track in the morning light. I had never before seen the mark of a carnivore so large. Jake sniffed at the print made in the dark soil. Then, whining faintly, his ears flattened against his head, he retreated behind me. I had never heard him whine before.

Trang looked about, studying the land ahead. "Thiu-Ta, we go now. We follow this great beast and learn from its movements what we must do to track it down and kill it. We move slowly. Keep your rifle close."

The land fell away before us toward a large valley between mountain ranges. I felt warmed and refreshed by sun and breeze.

We moved slowly as Trang followed tracks. Where the beast wandered away from the line of forward progress, my Montagnard tracker was able to project his forward movement and intercept the tiger's trail by walking stealthily in a straight line. This way we were able to close on the beast.

"We much closer to quarry now," Trang said. "We will use best caution. I think this is last day of travel before we begin to hunt."

I knew this meant we would be working the night shift.

I nodded.

We took up the trek again.

Night fell with no moonrise until the early hours. "I think we are very close now. We set ambush here. Tiger comes before morning."

"How do you know?"

"Tiger has tracked us. Now he begins hunt us. I know now it is male. Tonight, with luck, we see him."

Trang settled into a prone position under a frond. I dropped down beside him, Jake at my flank. It grew darker. I aimed my rifle generally down-range and looked through the night scope. We waited. The sounds of the night creatures grew louder.

I nodded off.

Jake emitted a low growl, waking me and bringing me to full alert. I looked through my night scope. I saw nothing. *Is Jake asleep and dreaming or did he sense something?*

A three-quarter moon rose throwing a dim light over all.

Except for a passing family of pigs, the rest of the night passed without incident.

Trang rose up at daybreak. "You must wait here for me Thiu-Ta. I will scout ahead and return soon."

As Trang disappeared into the underbrush, I sat cross-legged under a bush with my rifle across my knees. I thought of the tiger. *What will he be like? How fast can he move? Will he appear like my dream tiger?*

I heard a noise in the forest nearby.

Jake's wagging tail announced Trang's return. As he settled beside me, he removed a smallish jungle rat from a pocket and dropped it in front of Jake. The dog immediately pounced on the rat and began to devour it.

"Tiger is near. We are in his home range, village of Than Thuan, about two kilos from here. Soon we move to meadow nearby where he likes to hunt."

"Good. Let's go."

"No, too early. We must not give tiger time to smell us out."

"Okay. Yeah, that makes sense."

I set about cleaning my rifle. Jake decided to take an after-breakfast nap. Trang lounged against a tree, sucking on an unlit pipe.

"Tell me, Trang, have you killed many tigers?"

"No. I have seen many. The French hunted them for sport. They liked to ride on elephants. They hunted with high powered rifles while men like me scouted and flushed tigers out. A few of us were killed and eaten. These scars on my arms were made by embrace of a tiger. Most often tiger knew of our approach and disappeared into the mountains."

"Our tactic seems to be one of waiting in ambush for the tiger to come to us."

"Yes, if we want advantage, we must be set in position. When tiger appears we will have maybe one second to react. If you fast and accurate with your shot, we get to live and maybe kill the tiger. If not, tiger decides whether we live or die."

"What about this weretiger business?"

For the first time since the beginning of our hunt, Trang appeared unsure of himself.

"Thiu-Ta, I pray to your Christian God and to the Buddha and to my ancestors, that this is not the weretiger. If it is, we are dead . . . or worse. Now we must sleep while the sun is up."

I settled down in the brush to sleep. My mind kept coming back to what Trang said, "dead, or worse." I wanted to wake him and ask what he meant by "or worse."

I fell into a deep sleep and once again I dreamt of the tiger. His countenance grew until it occupied my entire mind. I could hear its hoarse breathing. In my field of vision, I saw him open his jaws to show gleaming fangs. Once again I was on the edge of a precipice, about to plunge into . . . I woke to Jake's licking my face and whimpering.

I sat up.

I was damp with perspiration despite the pre-dawn chill.

Trang was studying me with unreadable eyes. The sun was near the horizon.

"When you ready, we must go," Trang said.

He seemed not to possess any of his former friendliness, but was now distant and wary as he waited for me to collect my thoughts and gear.

Gotta get my shit together, I thought as I fought to rid myself of the fear I felt.

We moved slowly and cautiously, Trang leading, until the jungle foliage began to thin. He Stopped and dropped to one knee, signaling me to join him.

I knelt beside him.

Jake dropped to his belly at my knee.

Trang was studying the landscape to his front. All I could see was chest-high grass waving gently in the late-afternoon breeze.

"We wait. Tiger will come sometime after dark. We must be ready."

He looked at my rifle.

"You have special ammunition I gave you?"

"Locked and cocked and ready to rumble," I said with confidence I didn't feel.

Trang nodded and dropped to his belly, signaling me to do the same.

We waited. In the afternoon sun I heard Trang snoring lightly. Jake's back legs thrashed as he dreamt some dog dream.

The sun went down.

The grass stood silent. The air grew oppressive. The night creatures began to stir. I heard the clicking sounds of a troop of army ants as it passed in the near distance. The numerous callings of insects and animals large and small announced the commencement of the nightly pursuit of food. I listened for the sound of a tiger on its nightly hunt, not sure what that would be like. I looked through my night scope and saw nothing but tall grass.

Sometime during the night, I think I must have dozed a little. I was awakened by the sound of Jake's whimpering.

Fully awake now I looked through my night scope and saw nothing. Not sensing the nearness of Jake, I began to feel about. He was not there. I crawled toward where Trang was supposed to be. I called out under my breath. No response. Both of them were gone. I quickly resumed a firing position, and using the night scope, scanned the field. At the edge of panic now, I called, "Jake. Here boy. Here Jake. Where are ya, boy?" There was no answer.

What can I do? Where have they gone? I struggled for control. I wanted to run and I wanted to scream for

Jake and Trang. *Where the hell are you?* I forced myself to calm down.

Only one thing to do. Continue my vigil and wait until daylight.

I took up a prone firing position and resumed waiting for the tiger to appear.

I must not panic. I must continue until daylight.

I settled down and refused to think about what might have happened to Trang and to Jake. Every few seconds I looked through the night-scope until my vision wavered and blurred. I blinked and looked away for a few seconds and looked again into the scope.

I saw it.

A huge tiger filled the entire aperture of my scope. Its luminescent yellow eyes locked with my own as it drew nearer. Those eyes seemed to possess all the knowledge of the world. It stepped close, never taking its eyes off me. I tried to look away, to regain control of my faculties and focus on why I was here. I willed myself to pull the trigger, but could not break visual contact with the big cat.

The tiger held me captive in its gaze. Closer and closer it came. It seemed to engulf me. Then it began to purr. Its soft purring slowly morphed into a deep throated growl. Its mouth opened before my face to show its long pointed fangs. I stared into the bottomless chasm of its maw, mesmerized by the presence of such terrible beauty and power.

I lost my balance and fell. I tried to grasp onto something that would keep me from falling, but failed. I fell, turning and turning, into the chasm that was the body of this magnificent beast until at last I lost consciousness.

I awoke with a start to see what I thought must be an angel standing over me, completely engulfed in white. "Am I in Heaven?" I asked.

"No, not even close, Major. You're in the Pleiku Province Field Hospital. You've been here four days."

"But . . . what? . . . how?" I stammered, confused.

"Doctor will look in on you shortly. He'll be able to answer all your questions. Rest now. I'll arrange some food for you. You must be famished."

"I believe I could probably do a fair job on the south side of a cow headed north."

She laughed.

Oh Lord, I must be in love again.

I watched her leaving the tent.

Definitely in love again.

Later, while I was finishing up the last of a second steak, a Captain, looking very much like an Army doctor, entered. "Well, well. Looks like Lieutenant Connelly is taking good care of you."

At my quizzical look, the doctor added, "The duty nurse's name is Mary Connelly. I'm Doctor Anderson." He picked up a chart that hung at the end of my cot and studied it briefly. "Any pain at all?"

"No. None at all. Just a hell of a lot of questions starting with where am I and how did I get here?"

You're in the Field Hospital in Pleiku. A Dust Off (medivac) chopper crew brought you in last week. I gather they had been searching for you for some time.

Something about a dog showing up, obviously the victim of a tiger attack."

"Jake! Where is he?"

"Sorry, but the vet couldn't save him. Let's have a listen to your heart." He placed a stethoscope against my chest, and listened for a few seconds. Once again he picked up my chart and studied it.

"Right now the most important thing you need is rest. I'll drop by again tomorrow. Good night, Major."

Lying on my cot, I mourned poor Jake. He was such a faithful dog. I had hoped to take him Stateside with me. I fell asleep wondering what had happened to Trang.

I sensed I wasn't alone. I opened my eyes. The tiger stood beside my bed, staring at me.

Strangely, I was not afraid. I could hear his breathing quite clearly. His heart beat slowly, strongly, in time with my own. He gazed deeply into my eyes. I felt the familiar sensation of seeing myself reflected in the yellow irises of his eyes while, at the same time, seeing my face through his eyes.

The darkness began to slip away. I saw the corners of my tent clearly as if through a filter. All the sounds of the hospital were discernible. The odors were sharp and distinguishable—delicious. I could actually taste them. There was the smell of blood coming from the operating tent. Over there were the scents of Lieutenant Connelly preparing for bed.

I rose from my own cot and stood by the tiger.

I was the tiger.

As one, we left the tent and moved swiftly, silently away from the hospital. I skirted Pleiku, moving into the edge of the jungle.

The thoughts and movements of the tiger became indistinguishable from my own.

The sounds and smells of the forest were delicious.

I . . . we stood for long moments listening, savoring the sounds and the sights of the jungle throbbing with the activities of the night creatures, each on a hunt for food.

The rising moon cast long shadows through the forest.

I surged forward. It was time to hunt.

A SOLDIER'S DREAM

The moon is low
It shines weakly through the trees
The moon is low
My love lies by my side
Her warm breath on my neck
Tells me she is sleeping

I am at peace
Wind soughing lowly thru Pines
Sings a lullaby
Of yesterdays without war
I am at peace
The words are my mantra

The moon is low
It sings to me of hunting
A scent of blood is in the air
I shall not hunt tonight
Because my love
Lies close by my side

Angel

I stepped into the water with my rented surf board under my arm. I was surprised by the water temperature. Even at Wai Kiki I expected the Pacific to be cold, but it wasn't. I had never tried to surf before and was excited by the opportunity. I figured surfing couldn't be too difficult for a life-long skier. My wife was a good swimmer, but she demurred, preferring to watch from the shore.

I turned to look at Brenda sunning herself on the beach. She was so beautiful. I needed to reassure myself that she was really here. We had been apart for six months while I served in Vietnam. Now we were together for a week's rest and recuperation before I returned to the Central Highlands for a final six months to complete my second tour of duty.

My first tour in The Nam was rough. I'd experienced several close calls as a rifle platoon leader. Oh, there were the usual firefights we all faced; the bullets whipping by, the noise of the friendly artillery and enemy mortar falling close at hand.

When I say close calls, I'm talking about situations like, while walking in single file through the jungle, a Viet Cong mortar round landed close beside me. It picked me up and slammed me into the ground, leaving me with a concussion and a permanent ringing in my left ear. Bad luck you say, but I say not such bad luck as befell the soldier behind me and the one in front of me who were both killed by shrapnel from the round. Not a shard hit me!

Another time, after I'd been promoted to captain and was moved up to staff, I was supposed to be out of reach of such dangerous situations. I was riding back from a meeting in the passenger side of a jeep. I leaned over to retie my boot. As I did, several rounds crashed through the windshield. I straightened up to discover one of the rounds penetrated the windshield at eye level. Another round had killed the driver. I sustained no injuries when the uncontrolled jeep crashed.

I returned stateside after my tour feeling very lucky. I also felt I was living on borrowed time. Sooner or later my luck would run out. A second tour would kill me. I knew it.

When I received orders to return to Vietnam for a second year-long tour, I knew that I wouldn't return. I purchased a house for my wife and three children. I put my affairs in order so they'd be secure when I didn't return.

My orders sent me to a district advisor's job in Kontum, the heart of the Central Highlands and at the washout of the Ho Chi Minh Trail. My district was known as a "High Traffic Area."

My posting was to a lonely base camp half-way between the city of Kontum and the Laotian border. The people I was to work with were for the most part Montagnards, an aboriginal people who spoke no English. They didn't even speak Vietnamese.

My mission was to rebuild the district, most of which had been destroyed during the Tet offensive that year.

The situation was very iffy. Returning from Kontum city one day, early in my tour, I was accompanied by my interpreter and my dog. We intercepted what looked like a regional force company of about one hundred men. I stopped the jeep in the middle of the formation and told my interpreter to ask the unit commander what they were about. I hadn't heard of any maneuvers being conducted in this area.

My interpreter spoke with a first lieutenant who stopped at the jeep. They exchanged words I didn't understand.

"What did he say, Sergeant Trung?"

"Thiu-Ta, he say he has unit from Dak To. We go now!"

I looked about. The interpreter was clearly alarmed. The dog was growling. I stepped on the gas and moved out smartly.

"What was that all about?"

"They VC! We go fast!"

I stopped the jeep over the next hill, and after confirming with Kontum that no troops from Dak To were operating in our sector, called in helicopter gun ships to engage the VC.

The enemy was disbursed, but I was puzzled and I still don't know why they let me pass through their formation without killing me.

Apparently my luck was holding, but something was about to happen that would make me begin to wonder about the source of my luck. I was sitting in the trailer house that was my quarters and my office at Kontum District early one evening. I was preparing some periodic reports. After nearly an hour of hated paperwork, I felt the need to stretch. I got up and left my trailer. I looked in on the unit mess where my troops were watching a movie.

Not a minute after I left my quarters it was blown up. My trailer was completely destroyed. Had I not picked that moment to take a stretch, I would have been killed.

I looked up and down the beach as I entered the water. There were no other surfers around. I looked at the water. The tide was apparently going out. There was a slight rip in front of me moving toward my right. There didn't appear to be much surf up. That was good. I could paddle about and look good for Brenda without having to be good.

I paddled out and turned my board to face the beach. I looked over my shoulder to watch for a wave. There were none. Just a few swells. I saw that I was drifting seaward, but I wasn't worried. I should have been.

I started paddling toward shore. Suddenly a large swell lifted me up. My board began to speed toward shore, the swell building inexorably to a breaker. I didn't know what to do as I found myself on the forward face of a monster wave. The bow of the board pointed toward the bottom of the ocean. The wave broke and I was sent tumbling. The board was tossed into the air.

I surfaced and saw my board floating some distance away. I began swimming toward it. I was tired. The weight of my tee-shirt, worn to protect my back from the sun, began to drag me under. Lucky for me a surfer showed up and brought my board to me.

"Oh, thank you. I was really getting pooped."

"You're welcome."

I crawled aboard and paddled for nearly an hour before I made the beach.

"I was beginning to worry," Brenda said. "You were out there an awfully long time."

I stood on the beach and looked at the empty water.

"Did you see where he went?"

"Who?"

"The guy who brought my board back to me when that big wave hit me."

"Sweetheart, I didn't see anybody but you."

"Well he's gone now, but he was there when I needed help. I don't think I could have made it without him."

Brenda looked worried now.

"I've been right here the whole time. I didn't see anybody anywhere near you. We'd better get you out of the sun."

"Yeah, I'm pretty badly burned on the backs of my legs. Let's go get a tall cool one."

I thought no more about the incident until I was returning to Vietnam. During the long flight I had time to recount all the "lucky" things that had happened to me; things that seemed coincidental until the surfing incident.

I thought about the night, just a couple of weeks ago when, crossing the compound I had heard a 4.2 inch mortar round being fired from somewhere in Kontum.

Munitions of all kinds were launched all night long at varying intervals. We learned to distinguish between the various types of weapons. Whether they were friendly or enemy registered in our minds almost automatically.

Why I reacted to the friendly firing this time, I will never know. I stopped and waited for the round to land. A few seconds went by. I felt more than heard a "whoosh" and the round landed just beside me. It impacted the earth with a "thunk."

I was surprised I was still alive. If the round had exploded there would have been nothing left of me. If I hadn't stopped to wait for the impact, the round might have hit me.

The next day we dug up the projectile to discover one of the several safety pins that needed to be removed in order to arm each round was still in place.

Coincidence? Luck? Certainly it was lucky, but I was beginning to question its pure coincidence. I thought about the surfer at Wai Kiki and I wished I had paid more attention to him.

Then there was the incident with a grenade.

After my trailer was blown to bits, I began sleeping on a folding cot behind the radio shack. Because there was always someone on radio watch, I figured I'd have a ready-made personal guard to protect me while I slept, which wasn't often. Maybe two hours a day during siesta.

One night, I returned from a helicopter flight, overseeing a firefight in one of the villages.

I walked into the radio shack where Sergeant Sanchez was on radio watch.

"Anything happening, Sarge?"

"No sir. All is quiet for the time being."

"Good. Guess I'll take a nap. Wake me if a cricket farts."

"Sure thing, sir." The Sergeant laughed.

I walked back to my bunk. I relaxed and laid my head on my pillow and tensed. Someone had placed a hand grenade beneath it. I dared not move. I listened for the "ping" of the spring loaded handle or the faint "phzzz" of the fuse behind my head. A few seconds elapsed, seemingly like hours. I dared not move. Apparently, the grenade was not armed by the pressure of my head. I remembered that the VC set this kind of a booby trap by wrapping a damp rag around the handle and then pulling the pin. While the rag was wet, it would keep the handle from releasing the striker. Once released, the striker would swing and ignite the fuse. The grenade would explode in four seconds if it was American. Sometimes the VC set the fuse to go off immediately.

All these things raced through my mind as I pondered what to do.

"Sergeant Sanchez," I called softly.

"Yes sir."

"Don't say anything. Just get up quickly and get out. I'm lying on a grenade. It may go off. Get in the bunker."

"Roger that, sir. I'm gone."

When I knew the sergeant was safe, I rolled off the bunk onto the floor of the radio shack.

A minute went by and nothing happened. I rose to my feet, ran out of the shack and jumped into the bunker.

"Holy shit, sir. What's goin' on"

"Not sure. Maybe a booby trap. You wait here. I'll go see."

I returned to the radio shack and to my bunk. I lifted the pillow slowly to reveal a grenade wrapped in a rag, dry now. I carefully grasped the grenade. The handle was loosely attached.

I picked up the grenade, careful to keep the handle from flying off, and walked outside with it. Just beside the bunker was the mortar pit. I hesitated to drop the grenade into the pit because it might damage our 81mm mortar. I searched for alternatives. *Don't throw it. If there's no four second delay, you'll die. Drop it in. Better the mortar than you.*

I lay on the ground, next to the pit, reached out, and dropped the grenade into it.

It hit the bottom of the pit with a "thunk."

I waited a few minutes. Then I got up and went back to the radio shack.

"All clear, Sergeant."

Sanchez joined me in the shack.

"You get some sleep, Sergeant. I'll watch the radio. Can't sleep. Wait! Did anyone come into the radio shack during your shift?—except me, of course."

The sergeant thought for a moment, then shook his head.

"No sir. No one but Top Sweeney and he just stopped by to check on me."

The next morning I retrieved the grenade. I saw that the rag wrapped around it was a tattered VC flag. I exposed the grenade carefully, while holding the handle tightly against its body. *Now what do I do? I think I'll take a chance and throw it out onto the grass out of harm's way.*

I said a short silent prayer and heaved it onto the parade field. The rag flew off as well as the handle and the grenade landed with a conclusive "thunk."

Examining the grenade later, the explosive ordinance detachment concluded that the handle had moved enough to allow the striker to swing slowly and close on the fuse, but without enough torque to ignite the fuse.

The EOD lieutenant said, "You lucked out, Major."

Now, sitting in a jet speeding back to Vietnam, Brenda's aura still fresh in my consciousness, I began to put it all together. It wasn't luck or coincidence. I met my angel in the waters off Wai Kiki Beach. I was sure he'd let me know when my time was up. It wasn't to be soon.

I don't think I'll ever try to surf again. I'll stick to safer stuff like skiing and parachuting.

Mission Iditarod

When I arrived in Alaska in February of 1972, beginning a three year tour, I was briefed by the Brigade Commander, Colonel John Bender who became a lasting friend until his death some years later.

"Dick, the slot we have for you, operations officer, won't be vacant for a couple of months. Until then we have an exciting mission. You and I will be flying around tracing the historic Iditarod trail. Are you familiar with the story of Iditarod?"

"Can't say as I am, Sir."

"Well, grab us both a coffee and sit down. Let me fill you in."

I brought coffees from a pot I'd seen in the outer office and sat down to listen to what the Colonel had to say.

"In the early 1900s someone discovered gold in the town of Iditarod. It started a gold rush." The Colonel stood up and walked to a large map of Alaska on the wall. He pointed to a spot on the southern coast of Alaska to the west of Anchorage. "There it is, about 500 miles from here as the crow flies. It was a boom town for several years. Then when the gold petered out, everybody just closed their doors and went away. They had established a mail run overland by dog sled in winter and by wagon in summer. Today it's a ghost town. There's interest in having a sled dog race over the trace of the old trail. Our task is to find it."

My first job was to locate the home of Joe Redington Sr. and make plans for the Army to support his ground efforts to locate the trail. The first day I travelled over to the little town of Knik, across Cook Inlet from Anchorage, in a Jet Ranger, CH51 helicopter, flown by the chief of our brigade aviation section, Captain Charley Harris.

Charlie and I circled over Knik, a cluster of log buildings and trailers, some with smoke circling lazily from chimneys, all covered in a blanket of snow and looking deserted, on a sunny morning. The snow sparkled everywhere. It was a warm ten degrees.

I pointed at one larger building and said, "There's smoke coming from that building over there. Let's stop and ask directions to Redington's house."

"Yeah, looks like a roadhouse. Maybe we can get some lunch," Charlie said. (All eateries in rural Alaska are called roadhouses. Historically roadhouses were inns placed a dogsled's travel distance apart.)

"Sounds good. Looks like there's a parking lot beside the building."

Charlie nodded and set the ship down in the snow covered parking lot. The building, a two-story log affair, looked abandoned. Smoke rising from the chimney suggested otherwise.

We entered the front door, stomping the snow off our boots on a mat just inside the door. There was a collection of booths and a single bar. It appeared empty, but it was warm.

"Hello there, anybody home?" I called out.

A voice answered from beyond the bar, "Hello, hell yes I'm here. Be right with ya."

Charlie and I sat at the bar. A woman, robust and dressed in a warm-up suit, looking like an overweight wrestler, with a red and white checkered apron, walked in from the kitchen wiping her hands on a dish towel. She picked up three cups and a pot of steaming coffee and said, "Well, didn't expect to see anybody this morning. Did'ja fly in on that helicopter I heard a while ago? Ya want something ta eat?" She said all this in what sounded like a single sentence as she poured coffee for Charlie and me and one for herself. She shook both our hands and said, "Name's Lil."

"Yes, hello Lil. I'm Major Dick Dixon and this is Captain Charlie Harris." I took a sip of the steaming black brew, "I'd like a cheeseburger with everything on it. How about you, Charlie?"

He swallowed and said, "Sounds good to me."

"You boys over from the airbase?" She refilled our coffee cups and sat working on her own.

"No ma'am," Charley said. "We're from Fort Richardson."

"Oh well, Army, Air Force—it's all the same to me. Two cheeseburgers, works, coming up."

She returned to the kitchen and we heard her working at the grill. Soon the aroma of meat cooking filled the dining room.

She came back out with the coffee pot to refill our cups again.

I said, "Say, Lil, we're looking for a musher named Joe Redington. Do you happen to know where he lives?"

Immediately her look changed from friendly to combative. She picked up a cleaver from somewhere and began waving it around. "Joe Redington? Redington? Sure I know that dirty rotten son-of-a-bitch. And you, you bastards. Get outta here. Get out now before I get really mad." She stepped toward us, brandishing the cleaver.

I dropped a bill on the bar and we literally ran to the chopper.

"Holy shit." Charley said, throwing switches and revving up the engine, "What was that all about?"

"Search me. It appears she doesn't care much for Joe."

"That's putting it mildly. She's got a max case of cabin fever. Wish we coulda eaten the burgers before she threw us out," Charley said as he pulled pitch and we hopped up and over the surrounding cabins. I never did discover why she was so pissed off at Redington.

"Let's circle around a little," I said. "Maybe we can spot Redington's place. He's supposed to be a musher. There's gotta be a kennel or something showing the presence of dogs. Just stay away from the roadhouse. Lil's liable to throw that cleaver at us."

"Roger."

We circled the twenty or so snow covered cabins and trailers that comprised Knik.

I spotted a ramshackle trailer house surrounded by several mounds. "Hey, look. Those could be dog pens. It's the only place around that could be it. There's smoke coming from the chimney. Let's set her down."

Charlie settled the bird onto a nearby clearing. We dismounted and approached the trailer. A man stood in the doorway smoking a pipe. He looked to be about fifty. "Howdy," he said as we came up. He smiled, displaying several gaps in his teeth. I was reminded of Alfred E. Newman from Mad Magazine.

"I bet you're looking for me. I'm Joe Redington."

"Hello. My pilot and I were sent here by Colonel Bender at Fort Richardson to offer our help in finding the trace of the Iditarod trail."

"Well that's swell." He didn't sound like he was enthused about having the Army involved. "You can best help me by following my dogsled tracks and looking for other signs of the original trail. Tell me where I go wrong so I can correct and go on."

When I saw he had finished, I asked, "When will you start?"

"Already have. Should be in Skwentna by sometime next week. Just follow my tracks."

And that's how my Iditarod adventure began. I didn't know we were meeting with one of the more colorful characters in the history of Alaska. Joe was to become known as the father of the Iditarod Dog Sled Race.

I spent the rest of the winter until breakup (spring thaw) flying with Colonel Bender to different places along the old Iditarod Trail. Sometimes I'd spend time marking the trail on the ground with Joe Redington and his favorite dog team.

Together with Colonel Bender I visited Old Tom from Sucker Lake. Tom showed us the remains of a cabin he said marked the first night's stay on the way from Knik to Skwentna. I spent several days with Joe Delia checking his beaver trap line by snow machine along the Iditarod Trail running westward from Skwentna. We flew into villages like Nicholai and Mcgrath and interviewed people there who claimed to know where the trail trace really was. We concluded the trace varied from year to year depending upon weather and snow conditions. Erosion marks can still be seen from the air in places where the trail crossed the rivers.

Redington wanted the race to go to Nome on the coast of the Bering Sea, a thousand miles west. He reasoned no one had ever heard of Iditarod, so we'd get more publicity with Nome as the terminus.

This put the Army somewhat at odds with the mushers. Colonel Bender was more interested in Iditarod from a historic viewpoint. In fact we salvaged and carried a printing press from the ghost town of Iditarod by helicopter to Anchorage and placed it in the historic museum there during the summer of 1972.

In March of that year I took over as Brigade Operations Officer. A few months later Colonel Bender received orders to the lower 48 and was relieved by Colonel Rufus Lazelle.

The next winter, one of our rifle companies skied from Knik to Iditarod on an adventure training exercise. Someone years ago had authorized the purchase of twenty or thirty single-skied Canadian snow machines from Ski-doo. They were old and broken-down, larger and slower than the more popular, lighter weight Arctic

Cats most civilians used in the middle 1970s. (In the lower 48 snow machines are called "snow mobiles.")

Every few years the Army ran a test program attempting to show snow machines could serve a useful tactical role. My job as 172d Brigade Operations Officer under a new brigade commander was to resurrect the issue.

During the summer of 1972 I studied the history of field trials the machines had undergone. One common thread ran through the reports. The Army conducted each of its tests with the Ski-Doos loaded down with machine guns, trailers, and other weighty paraphernalia. I opined if we kept the machines stripped of all equipment and if we bought some newer, faster, and quieter machines with double skis for better steerabilty, we could make good use of them for long range reconnaissance missions.

Termination dust (Alaskan for first snow of the season) fell on the Chugach Mountains just east of Fort Richardson in September of 1972. Things began to heat up vis-à-vis the possibility of mushing to Nome in March.

Colonel Lazelle was invited to attend several Iditarod Race committee meetings in downtown Anchorage.

He briefed me after one such meeting in January, 1973.

"Dick, it looks like this sled dog race is actually going to happen. I've committed us for helicopter support to assist in marking the trail. Can you think of any additional help we can provide?"

"Right off hand I don't know, sir. Give me a few days to put the staff on it and I'll see what we can come up with."

A few days later I presented a report of our studies to Colonel Lazelle.

"Briefly, sir, we believe a snow machine that runs quietly and is light enough to be lifted by Huey could fill a real gap in our winter operations.

"If we mounted an expedition from here to Nome using the old Bombardier Ski-doos and following the track made by the dogsled teams, we could prove it can be done. We can capitalize on the publicity the race is sure to draw."

"Do you think those old junks can make it?"

"We have twenty-four of the machines. Seventeen of them are currently running. If we use a dozen of the machines on the trail, we can cannibalize the others for replacement parts and fly them in by chopper. We can refuel by bladder dropped by chopper, and resupply all along the way."

"That's a good plan. But why not take it a step further and offer to break trail for the mushers?"

"Sir, that's not a good idea. My plan calls for abandoning one or more machines if need be along the trail to be policed up later. If just one dog team passes a disabled snow machine, we'll be the laughing stock of Alaska."

"You've got a point. When would you plan to start?"

"About two weeks after the mushers finish."

"Make your plans. We'll put two men on each Ski-Doo. Let's see . . . plan for relief of each soldier every 200 or so miles or by the day, whichever you think best.

"Contact the Bombardier factory in Quebec. Find out how many parts they have lying around that will fit these machines and how soon we could have them. We'll send our twin engine airplane to pick them up if necessary."

"Roger, sir. I'll get right on it." Hot Damn! I was energized. The Old Man had bought my plan.

A few days later, Colonel Lazelle called me into his office.

"Dick, I briefed the general on your plan. He approves it with one change. He has committed us, to the race committee, to break trail for the mushers."

"All the way to Rainy Pass, sir?"

"All the way to Nome. Let's get on it, Major. Oh, by the way. No dog will pass an Army snow machine on the trail. Do you understand?"

"Roger, sir." I was chagrined. This news put a different slant on things. Nevertheless, I was determined to be successful.

My staff and our support battalion scrambled to make ready for D-Day which was set for fourteen days prior to the start of the race, sometime in the middle of March, 1973. We stockpiled spare parts and prepared fuel and food rations for the trail. I held strategy meetings with my staff. We war gamed all the bad things that could happen and made contingency plans to solve any problems. When it came to the issue of dogs overtaking our machines, I knew my job depended on preventing that.

"I suggest we drop frozen salmon along the trail to distract the dogs," Lieutenant Ed Popek, one of my liaison officers, said.

"Why not poison the salmon, not enough to kill. Just enough to make the dogs sick and slow 'em down a little," my Chemical Warfare Officer, Captain Derry offered.

"We ought to introduce female dogs in heat, every so often on the trail. That ought to slow them down." My assistant operations officer, Captain Ortiz was only half joking.

I worked harder on planning this mission than I ever had, even for combat missions in Vietnam. My job and my reputation in Alaska were at stake.

On D-day at H-hour, we were ready to go. Depending on the reliability of the Ski-doos, which was zero, I planned for the machines to be able to make fifty miles a day through trackless wilderness. I figured the dogs could make at most fifty miles a day on good track. If all went as planned we should make Nome at least a week ahead of the dogs.

Aviation and support units were leaning forward in the saddle. Unfortunately, so was the weather. During the two weeks before the race started, record snowfall fell in the Susitna Valley, running generally north and south for 100 miles to the west of Anchorage.

The Ski-Doos left Fort Richardson on time. One machine broke down before leaving the post. We were able to replace it immediately with another.

We ran along the Richardson highway bypassing Palmer. We turned left along the road to Wasilla, then south at the head of Cook Inlet and down to Knik, where we spent the first night. I warned the officer in charge to stay away from the Knik Roadhouse.

The next few days we ran across the Susitna River and north to Skwentna. The snow was so deep we had to break trail by foot with shovels. A day out of Skwentna we were averaging less than twenty miles a day in record breaking snow depths. I sent a patrol on skis to range forward of the Ski-Doo teams marking and breaking trail ahead of the machines. I joined the ski patrol periodically for a day or two.

By day three it didn't look good. We were facing constant break-downs and uncooperative weather. The maintenance crews were kept working around the clock. We replaced three machines in Skwentna. When the race started we were barely through Rainy Pass in the Alaska Range.

Less snow had fallen on the western slopes of the pass. The going was easier and we made better time to Nickolai and McGrath. Once through the Kuskokwim Mountains onto the flats toward Ophir, it was easier finding helicopter refueling and resupply sites. We were still replacing an average of one machine a day as the maintenance crews continued their hard work. Huey helicopters, straining under the weight, would deliver replacement snow machines and retrieve broken down machines several times daily.

From Kaltag, Reddington and Mackey had marked the trail to Unalakleet. The crews rested a bit at Kaltag as I flew over the leaders of the race leaving Ophir. Our machines were, at best, three days ahead of the lead dogs.

I began to sweat it. I stayed with the machines skiing sometimes in front, sometimes trailing the snow machines between Ophir and Unalakleet. In no case were we able to get all twelve snow machines running at the same time.

From Unalakleet we made good time to Shaktoolik. From there we traversed the sea ice of Norton Bay to Moses Point praying we wouldn't run into any overflows. We gained almost a day on the mushers who were required to register at their checkpoint in Koyuk at the head of Norton Bay. They would move faster when they reached the ice.

We prayed the weather would hold the rest of the way into Nome.

It socked in and the wind blew from Moses Point to Dickson. We felt our way, marker to marker for a day. The dogs were closing rapidly. I spent the last three days of the trip making sure there were no machines left on the trail.

Colonel Lazelle flew to Nome and together we met the snow machines at the finish line. A crowd of some fifty people had gathered to cheer them into Nome. One by one, I counted them until I got to ten. I thought of Colonel Bender and wished he could be here. I showed the men to the National Guard armory where we were to spend the night before returning by air to Fort Richardson.

Captain Jack Keane (now a retired four star general and candidate for Secretary of Defense. one of the finest men I've ever served with), the leader of the snow machine expedition at this time radioed to tell me he was with a machine broken down between Dickson and Nome. He understood there was a Huey on the way with parts, but the lead dog was just hours away.

Charley Harris called in to tell me he was circling the two remaining machines.

"Charley, can you tow the broken machine with your chopper to just outside Nome to give the parts bird time to arrive?

"Dunno, it's never been done, but I'll give it a try."

We towed the machine some twenty miles until the Huey arrived with repair parts. I was really sweating it now.

Two hours later, the last two machines crossed the finish line together, followed by the lead dog just fifteen minutes later, mushed by Dick Wilmarth, an Alaskan from Red Devil who finished in twenty days.

The National Guard commander met us at the armory and showed us over to the Board of Trade where we ordered beer all around.

As far as I know some of the hulks of the Ski-Doos are still sitting at the Nome Airport.

Back at Fort Richardson the next day, I reported to Colonel Lazelle with my after-action report.

"Great job, Dick. I think we made our point with the Pentagon. Combat Developments Command has agreed to do further studies on the tactical use of snow machines. Take a break.

Finland on Skis

Three of us were holed up in a resort hotel in the middle of the winter, somewhere in Finland during the winter of 1979. We were on the shore of what must in summer be a beautiful lake. Now it was frozen and covered with snow. Ski trails traversed it for miles. It was beautiful. It was cold, but not forbiddingly so. And the dry air gave everything a crisp feeling.

We three were on a state department visit and tour of military facilities in Finland. We had flown in to Helsinki several days before and toured several locations by van before being taken to the hotel for the weekend. Leader of the group was Colonel Spalding from Headquarters Department of the Army at the Pentagon. He was in the Quartermaster Corps, a REMF (Rear-echelon Mo-----Fu----), but a pleasant man. The second of our trio was Major Waldenburger from Training Command Headquarters at Fort Monroe, Virginia. He was a German born, naturalized American. I immediately disliked his know everything attitude. I suspected both men were on a boondoggle.

As an infantry major, I was assigned to the Army in Alaska to write doctrine for fighting in winter. As such, I was the only one who qualified for the trip as having winter expertise. My mission was to discover how the Finnish Army fought in the snow. Oh yes, I was on a boondoggle, too.

We were to spend the weekend at what can only be described as a posh hotel, catering to those who enjoyed water sports in summer and ice and snow activities in winter. As with most of the country, it was jam-packed with gorgeous women and old frost-bitten men.

While I was settling in, the phone rang. It was Colonel Spalding. "Want to join Major Waldenburger and me in the sauna at 1700?"

We finished every day with the sauna in one form or another. The previous day we had participated in a regimental sauna at lakeside. We plunged into a hole that was chopped through the more than twenty-four inches of ice on a lake. The experience was totally invigorating. We rolled in the snow, naked as jays, (though I must confess I've never seen a live jay bird with no feathers), and then took a hot shower before participating in drinking vodka.

"Certainly, Sir. I'll see you there," I said,

At the appointed hour, I found my way to the sauna which proved to be a private lounge with sauna room and shower surrounding an olympic sized pool. All was white marble and clean as a hospital. We seemed to have the place to ourselves. What a fine time we had. The attendant took our orders for appetizers in between and after sauna. As was customary, we first showered, then sat naked, sweating in the sauna as long as we could stand it. Then we showered again, and clad only in towels, like Romans, sat about in the lounge eating wurst and a kind of crumpet. When we were completely rested we again enjoyed the heat of the sauna. When I'd had enough I ran out of the sauna, and plunged into the pool.

When I surfaced I realized the pool was surrounded by several sauna suites, just like ours. I saw windows, behind which were Finns, men and women, all applauding my performance.

Abashed, I beat a hasty retreat, attempting to protect the family jewels from any more exposure.

Later, I visited the sumptuous bar. The bartender asked in faultless American English, "What'll it be for you, sir?"

"I'd like a screwdriver, please."

"I'm awfully sorry sir. I don't know what a screwdriver is. Can you coach me?"

"You don't know what a screwdriver is?" I started to tell him that it was the national drink of Ballard, but knowing he'd not know Ballard, a suburb of Seattle with a predominately Scandinavian population, I said, "Just throw a shot of Finlandia into a whiskey glass with ice and orange juice."

As the bartender followed my instructions, I noticed several people in the bar followed the proceedings intently.

"Try this, sir and tell me if this is what you intended," said the barkeep.

Noticing that I had an audience, I theatrically took a sip. Raising my hand, I closed my eyes and said, "Ah-h-h. Fantastic. Best screwdriver I've had all day!"

Right away everyone in the bar ordered a screwdriver. Thus it was that I lay claim as the American who introduced the screwdriver to Finland.

Next morning as we three Americans were enjoying a fine breakfast, our Finnish Army guide, Major Daljorrg, joined us and asked, "Gentlemen, do you know how to Ski-jor?"

Each of us responded that we did.

I had ski-jored in Alaska and in the previous year while on winter maneuvers with the Norwegian Army. Ski-joring was a way of moving a group of soldiers across the snow, holding on to a rope and being pulled on skis behind a tracked vehicle. I was accustomed to speeds of up to fifteen miles per hour. The Norwegians could maintain this speed for up to eight hours and eat their lunch on the move.

"Very good," said Major Dahljorrg. "You'll be picked up at lakeside this afternoon at 1500. From here you will ski-jor across the lake to an assembly area where you will join one of our units for a three-day exercise. You've been issued skis, boots, and poles. If you need anything else let me know now. Any questions?"

"Will we return here?" I asked.

"Yes, you may leave everything you won't need for the exercise in your rooms. It will be safe, I assure you. Any other questions?"

When there were none, the major stood up and said, "Good. I'll see you in three days."

I spent the rest of the day relaxing in the luxury of the hotel and making notes for my after-action report.

During our in-briefing to Finland, I was most impressed by the fact that Finland's national defense strategy seemed not to have changed since World War II. It consisted primarily of a dependence on dismounted light infantry defending in the woods. I was also surprised to hear that Finland had a national conscription policy.

The general staff appeared proud of the fact that while Finland had considered itself in league with the Axis during the war, they were the only country in the pact not to declare war on the United States.

That Finland had a mutual defense pact with Soviet Russia was interesting, particularly during these latter days of the cold war. Their attitude about that was expressed dourly by one officer who said, "We don't like to have our farmers work too close to the border for fear one might trip and fall. We expect the entire Soviet Army might rush across the border to help him up."

Later in the day we visited the military academy and the home of General Mannerheim, Finland's national hero and their version of our General Washington. Approaching the academy, I noticed an antique piece of artillery placed so as to point directly at the front door of the building. I said to our guide, "It's very unusual to see a cannon pointed essentially to the rear."

"Well," said major Dahljorrg, "If we turn it about so it's facing away from the building, it will point directly at Soviet Russia, a violation of our treaty which might well be considered provocative."

The next day we traveled by van northward to the town of Lahti. I was impressed by the flatness of the terrain. There were no mountains in sight, just miles of forest and thousands of lakes. There was a firing range near Lahti where soldiers were practicing firing at tank silhouettes. We were shown about by the local infantry battalion commander who was quite outspoken in his disdain for the Russians.

I said to him, "I notice that the silhouettes look a lot like Russian T-34s."

"Indeed they do," the Finnish lieutenant colonel replied, "but when the Russians are visiting we change the silhouettes to look like American M-48s."

That evening, while enjoying cocktails at the regimental mess in Lahti, I continued the discussion I had begun earlier on the range with the Finnish light colonel. "So I notice that many of you Finnish speak almost perfect American English. Do you also speak Russian?"

"I can only speak for myself," he replied with a wry smile. "I only speak one word of Russian but I find that one word is all I need to get by."

"Really. What word is that?"

"Rookyvaar!"(sic) he answered.

"Rookyvaar? What does that mean?"

"Hands up!" We had a good laugh together, but I've never been sure he was joking.

Later, after dinner, we three Americans attended a reception for the regimental commander and his wife in the room where Mannerheim had held meetings with Hitler and his cronies. I felt strange sitting in an overstuffed chair and looking up at a picture of the same grouping of furniture, seeing Hitler, Goering, Goebels, and others. Goebels had been sitting where I sat now. I remember thinking; *I hope they've at least changed the upholstery covering.*

After the formalities a young man appeared pushing a wheeled cart holding bottles of liquor. The colonel's wife, with whom I was speaking at the time, smiled, "May I offer you a drink, Major?"

"Certainly, Ma'am."

"What would you like?"

"Vodka with a little ice would be nice."

Searching about the cart and finding no vodka, she immediately gave orders to the young man who sped away, returning with a bottle of Finlandia.

"Ah, my favorite kind," I said.

"I must apologize, Major. We didn't think you Americans drank vodka."

"No apologies needed, Ma'am. Americans drink most anything," I said raising my glass to her.

I woke suddenly, not realizing I'd dropped off. The clock showed twenty minutes before we were to leave. I dressed hurriedly, grabbed my skis and poles, and went outside. Waiting at lakeside were three snow mobiles. I went over to shake hands with the drivers and introduce myself. Only one of them spoke English. My two American partners showed up and after introductions, we each paired up with a snow mobiler.

Colonel Spalding led off, followed by Major Waldenburger (I'd taken to calling him Major Shicklegruber, the rumored real name of Adolf Hitler.) He didn't appreciate it, but the Finns saw its humor). I brought up the rear, hanging on for dear life and limb, as the machines were traveling at top speed, better than twenty miles an hour. Fortunately the lake surface was very smooth. We were wearing Finnish Army issue skis. They had no metal edges, so we couldn't steer them on the frequent bare patches of ice. The driver looked back frequently to see how I was doing. Each time he did, I'd give the water-ski signal to slow down. He read this as a signal to go faster.

Soon we passed Major Schicklegruber who had taken a tumble. I worried that he might be hurt. A little farther on we passed Colonel Spalding attempting to get to his feet. Now I was in the lead and determined to keep my footing. We sped on across the lake, stopping only after we had reached the wood line on the opposite shore.

Two soldiers appeared, skiing out of the trees, to guide us to the assembly area. They set a fairly fast pace as we set out. The snow was hard-packed at two or three feet deep with about two inches of new powder on top. There was no wind, overcast skies, temperature in the twenties; ideal for touring.

The secret to traveling comfortably on foot over the snow is the layering of clothing so it can be donned or doffed, regulating body temperature and preventing over-heating and perspiring. If you get overheated, when you stop and the sweat turns cold, you risk becoming a cold casualty. At best you'll be very uncomfortable.

I wore G.I. woolen long-johns with a woolen sweater and a nylon windbreaker over all. In a day-pack, I carried another woolen sweater and a heavy canvas parka. I waited for a rest stop to remove my windbreaker. When I realized that, like the Norwegians, the Finns weren't much for rest stops, I doffed my jacket on the move.

We skied for about two hours over level ground through deciduous forest. The going was fairly easy on foot, but I began to understand how tanks and other tracked vehicles could be canalized by cutting the trees so the trunks interlocked forming an abatis. Defending thusly, the tanks would be forced into single file and could be defeated one a time.

At length we arrived in an assembly area where the battalion had established a defensive line and pitched yurt-like tents. Unlike Americans who, when they stop, are always digging in, the soldiers had taken up positions behind rocks and trees. Also, unlike Americans, they built fires for cooking and warmth. They had a way of building a fire using three logs staked on top of each other to maximize heat while minimizing light. I have tried to emulate this method on several occasions, but failed, probably because I had no access to the hard woods of the Finnish forest.

We enjoyed wurst cooked over the fire and vodka, another difference from the American Army which never drinks alcohol in the field. A highlight of the evening occurred when the battalion commander called a private soldier over to the fire from his position behind a nearby rock outcropping. The soldier dropped to one knee by the fire, pulled a paper from his jacket pocket, and began to read a poem in Finnish. The battalion commander translated. The colonel told us the soldier's grandfather had written the poem while occupying that same position during the Russian War (their name for the Russo-Finnish war in 1940).

That night we slept in the relative comfort of a heated tent with a soldier on fire-watch.

The next morning we moved out through the quiet of the forest, the only noise was the "shush" of our skis through the snow. I had no idea what our mission was. Where we were going or what we were going to do when we got there, remained a mystery. We skied for three days and nights without a single stop. The only remarkable thing about the whole experience was the unchanging aspect of the wooded terrain. At the end of our trek we found ourselves back near the hotel. We enjoyed a sauna, after which we dressed and were driven to the headquarters of the unit with which we had maneuvered, for a fine dinner.

Next day we loaded up in the van and headed back to Helsinki and the Hotel Intercontinental. It had been a fine adventure and I vowed to spend another winter ski touring in Finland.

Encounter

I stood on the shores of a wild lake on the Alaskan Peninsula, casting a spoon into the leading elements of a red salmon run, just in from the sea. Each cast resulted in a strike of an eight to ten pound rompin', stompin' sockeye salmon.

I played it until it tired and I was able to land it. Then I carefully withdrew the hook, and released the beautiful silver-sided fish as the law required. I was in protected waters, and so was allowed to possess only one fish.

Because I came to the Brooks River, in the Katmai National Monument, to catch a trophy Rainbow trout, I released everything else I caught.

It was the dark of a June night. The darkest I could expect, during the Alaskan summer, still allowed me to see silhouettes against the moonless sky.

I heard footsteps approaching, splashing though the water along the shore of the rocky beach.

Now who is this coming? I better let him know I'm here.
"Hey, hello there."

Whoever was walking toward me, along the shore, stopped and stood silent.

Then I saw, silhouetted against the midnight sky, the form of a great Brown Bear, standing at least ten feet tall on his hind legs, not a dozen feet away.

My breath caught in my throat.

I looked up at the dark form of this mighty creature silently contemplating me.

I froze, then dropped my fishing rod onto the beach, and said quietly, "O—o—h, it's you. Pardon me."

Backing slowly away from the shore, I entered the wood line and popped into my tent.

The bear didn't follow. He was, I supposed, more interested in the school of salmon that was beginning its run through the lake.

I was relieved to hear his splish . . . splash, as he continued his trek up the beach.

Of the many encounters with various bears during my time in Alaska, I have to say that bears, while intimidating, are not the most dangerous critters in the land.

Moose are the most unpredictable, and among the biggest of the Alaskan animals. One minute you're walking quietly through the woods, the next minute you face a charging 2,000 pound bull-moose. There's no facing down a charging moose, and maybe there's no way to avoid it. Because of its unpredictable nature, I consider it to be the most dangerous animal in Alaska.

The strangest and scariest encounter I experienced, during my eight year sojourn in Alaska, happened one gray day that promised snow. It occurred on the military reservation at Fort Richardson, in the foothills of the Chugach Mountain Range, near Anchorage.

It was Thanksgiving Day. My wife had a turkey roasting in the oven. I decided rather than sit around smelling the feast being prepared, stomach grumbling, I'd go for a short ski.

The previous night's weather had offered an inch of powder on a solid base of a yard of more of compact snow. The morning offered ideal conditions for cross-country skiing.

I asked if any of my children wanted to come with me for a quick workout. They all preferred to sit around smelling the turkey cooking. My dog, The Bummer, usually eager to hit the trail, was also reticent this day.

I stepped out on the back porch. The temperature was hovering around 20 degrees Fahrenheit, perfect for a morning's ski. I waxed for dry snow conditions and slipped into my bindings. I slipped the straps of my poles on my wrists and set off at a heart-quickening tempo onto a trail that circled the post for some twenty miles.

The aroma of roasting turkey was still in my nostrils as I glided the first five miles through lightly wooded terrain. Near the foothills of the mountains, I slowed to a more sedate pace, better suited to the fifteen miles or so I decided would be a good pre-dinner workout for me today.

I settled into a solid, mile-eating rhythm, and was lulled nearly to somnolence by the sound of the snow against my skis. Rime frost built up on my face and on the lenses of my goggles.

I continued climbing toward the base of the mountains. My pace slowed as the open woods gave way to thicker brush. After an hour I stopped to drink from my OJ-bottle and to take a short breather.

The forest was wrapped in winter silence. No birds were about. As my breathing subsided, I looked around at the snow covered trees. It was beautiful, and oh so peaceful here in the woods. I thought about bears. Then laughed aloud as I remembered all the bears were asleep now, deep in hibernation. Still, the hairs were standing up on the back of my neck. I was being observed.

I looked around and spotted a small dog. It stood absolutely still, not moving, except for its tongue hanging out, moving up and down with each breath which floated visibly on the chilled air. Its eyes were locked with mine in an expression I found unsettling and strangely foreboding.

My first inclination was to drop to one knee and call to the dog. Standing in my path, it wasn't inherently threatening. However, nothing about the dog spoke of connection with humans. This seemed unnatural in a canine, and more than a little sinister. Its tail was held rigid. It appeared to be studying me.

Spooked now, I decided to head for home. Swiveling on my skies, I swung my head to keep my eyes on the dog. It stood, silently regarding me.

I set off at a pace that would soon tire me. I slowed down into a rhythm I knew I could maintain indefinitely. Mounting a low summit, I raced down the other side.

I glanced over my shoulder to discover the dog was keeping pace with me. Only now he was joined by another, larger, and more wolf-like dog.

Startled by this new and more threatening pursuer, I crossed my tips and nearly fell. Pitching forward I managed to catch my balance. Instinctively I knew that to fall would bring more danger.

I stopped and turned my upper body so I faced the dogs. They were closer now. They approached to within a few yards and stood quietly, intimidating me.

My inclination, because I am at heart a dog lover, was to call to them. I knew, instinctively, they would not respond. I turned forward and moved on. I spotted, in my peripheral vision, a third dog moving up to join what was rapidly becoming a hunting pack of feral dogs.

Understanding now that my life was in danger, I began skiing swiftly toward the post. I was on the edge of panic. I knew I needed to slow my pace or risk a fall.

I glanced to the rear. The dogs were keeping pace with me.

They moved silently, like wraiths through the trees. I found their silence more fearsome than their barking or howling would have been.

Now I saw there were six of them, spread out in a semi-circle, and closing on me.

Winded, I leaned on a tree to rest and gather myself.

Looking back, now there were seven of them quietly watching me. They were closer than before.

Growing angry now, I swung a ski-pole through the air and shouted, "Get outa' here, ya bastards! I'll break your necks! Shoo! Git!"

They comprised several different cross-breeds, some big and some not so big. Together they posed a formidable threat if they decided to attack.

They didn't move. As one they stood and stared me down. Their tongues lolled and their lower jaws hung open, revealing their fangs. They joined in a silent sinister phalanx.

Now I was really, really scared. I tried to think about how far I needed to go to reach the cantonment area of the post. It couldn't be far.

I shouted desperately, "Hello! Anybody there? Hey! Help!"

My cries were muffled by the snow-covered trees.

I felt foolish calling for help, threatened by a few dogs.
No one answered.

I studied the canines.

They studied me.

I knew my only defense was to flee.

I skied as fast as I dared down the trail whence I had come, caught a ski-tip in a bush and sprawled on my belly.

The pack closed in.

They were snarling and growling now as they circled me. I rolled onto my knees, and waved my poles about as weapons, trying to keep them at bay.

The largest of them, the wolfish looking cur swept in, striking for my throat. Using a ski-pole like an epee against his fangs, I fended him off, aiming at his eyes.

Growling, he backed off and gathered himself for another lunge.

I knew I had to get to my feet now or I would surely be dog food at the end of day.

I Gathered my strength, faced the fiercest of the dogs and, baring my teeth, growled my best Ranger growl. At the same time I waved my ski poles menacingly.

The dogs backed away a few paces. I put my hands under me and pushed myself upward. I had only one chance and was done for if I faltered.

I made it. The dogs backed still more and grew suddenly silent. They stood watching, apparently waiting for me to fall.

I began to ski. I moved slowly, methodically, so as to be sure I did not lose my footing.

The dogs followed, now at a respectful distance, as we entered the housing area.

I recognized the back of my own house.

I stopped and looked back.

The dogs were gone. The woods were silent. Snow was starting to fall.

I smelled the turkey cooking inside the house. I had made it. I kicked off my skis and entered the safety of my own home.

My wife hugged me and said, "We were worried that you might be late for dinner."

My dog, sensing my fading fear, sat attentively at my feet looking up at me letting me know in his own way, he loved me. He sniffed inquisitively at my pant legs and growled softly.

I sat at table, joined hands with my family, and asked God's blessing of the meal.

I thank God for giving me the strength to save myself from the feral dogs.

Of the many encounters I have had with the wild creatures that inhabit Alaska, none were as sinister or menacing as this chance encounter with dogs gone wild. I vowed never to be caught so alone and so helpless again.

NIGHT VISITOR

It was late November. Winter cold had settled in the mountains. Soon it would snow. A full moon reflected in black and silver tones on the rocks above timberline. From the shadow of an outcropping, a creature stepped into the moonlight. It was the only thing moving in the night. It walked upright like a man, but moved with the grace of a wild being.

Stopping in the moonlight, the creature stood motionless for long moments. It tested the slight wind coming up from the valley below. Short plumes of steam, caused by the cold air, emanated from its distended nostrils. Its head was totally covered by long shaggy hair. Its eyes were two black holes.

Very soon the mountain steeps would be choked by the yearly blizzards. The creature knew it would very soon be driven to seek shelter somewhere below the timberline.

It picked its way down the mountain slowly at first. Then, driven by some unknown impetus, the creature fairly loped toward the valley below.

Every so often it would stop, look around, and test the air for signs of—something.

The creature slowed as it reached timberline and to thread its way carefully among the trees, leaving no tracks. It stopped and, raising its head, picked up the scent of smoke. Moving forward again, silently, the creature seemed to be familiar with its surroundings.

Far below, in the valley, the lights of a solitary cabin could be seen. White smoke, reflected in the moonlight, could be seen coming from its chimney. The creature seemed to be drawn to it.

"Sure is gettin' cold out there," said Tom. "Might be a three-dog night."

"Sure hope not," Jesse responded. "Only got two dogs and none to spare."

Both men laughed at the inside joke. They had been close friends for many years and shared many memories.

Tom had ridden his horse up the mountain that day. He planned to spend the weekend with Jesse before returning back down to town and his job at the mercantile store.

He always rode his horse up to visit with Jesse, because that's the way he'd always done it, even after he'd been able to afford his Chevy truck. Riding up to the cabin was like going back in time to simpler days. Now it was almost a ritual.

Jesse had decided to stay on at the cabin after Rachel died. *Shame it had to happen while Billy was gone.* Together they'd home schooled their son and only child. Jesse had continued on even after young Billy had grown and gone off to the Army.

Whenever Tom went to the cabin he felt as if he was entering an area where time stood still.

They sat together in front of fire in a large stone fireplace. Jesse's two old hounds, Maggie and Dicken, slept at his feet. The fire crackled and threw sparks every now and then. The lantern remained unlit. Both men smoked their pipes and relaxed in the warmth of the fire. Beside each of them sat glasses of half-sipped homemade whiskey, distilled in the summer by Jesse.

"Wish you'd kick that dog in the ribs," said Tom. "He's snorin' like a trooper. Can't hear myself clickin' my store-bought teeth."

Jesse nudged Maggie with his toe. The dog sat up, stretched, and then flopped down and started to snore again.

"That's the best you're gonna get," said Jesse, stoking his pipe, "Take your teeth out. Maybe that'll help." Again they laughed together and sipped a bit more of the whiskey.

"Think I'll put another log on," said Tom, rising to light the lantern. "Then I think I'd better go out to the barn and check on ol' Buster. That horse is gettin' too old to take the cold the way he used to."

"Sure, you bet'cha. Don't forget to bring in an armload of firewood on yer way back."

Tom donned his jacket and left for the barn. The dogs lifted their heads simultaneously and watched him go out. Again in cadence they dropped their heads and went back to sleep. Jesse studied the flames of the fire and thought about Billy. The loneliness crept in. Billy had been gone for almost a year now. He returned from the war in more-or-less one piece, but something was missing.

The young man had been close to his mother and always made sure to celebrate her birthday in some way. He had left to go to war before her last birthday and only returned after her death. Jesse expected that Billy would mourn, but there was something more . . . or less. The boy let his hair grow long, stopped shaving, and rarely cleaned

122

up. He often left the house on long hunting trips in the high mountains accompanied only by his dog, Skipper.

Last year when he killed a bear, he skinned it out and began wearing the hide like an Indian or a caveman. He stayed away from home for increasingly longer times. He seemed more than a little like the wild critters he hunted. Jesse missed him greatly and watched daily for his return.

One day he returned carrying the body of Skipper. Draped across Billy's shoulder was the hide of a cougar that apparently had killed the dog. Billy never said. Just buried Skipper in the back field. Something of himself, it seemed, he buried along with the dog. Two days later he disappeared and hadn't returned.

That was last spring. With the coming of his mother's birthday, Jesse expected his return.

The door of the cabin opened, rousing Jesse from his ruminations. The dogs re-awakened. Dicken sat up and scratched behind one ear. Tom entered stamping his feet and shucking his boots by the door. In his arms he held three large fir logs.

"Damn! She's a cold one for sure!" he said, adding his load to the logs piled by the fireplace and placing the lantern nearby.

Tom moved his seat closer to the fire and resumed sipping his whiskey.

"Horse okay?" asked Jesse, picking up his own glass.

"Yuh. I put a blanket over him. He was a bit skittish though, I think there might be a cougar about. We'll want to keep our ears open. I'll check on him after a while.

"Where do you think Billy is tonight?"

"Dunno. Now that winter's on us and it'll snow soon, I expect to see him any time. In fact, I wouldn't be surprised if he showed up tonight."

Neither man spoke. Both of them studied the fire. The night grew colder. Jesse put another log on the fire and poured two more whiskeys.

The silence was broken by the whinnying of the horse. The noise aroused them from their wool-gathering by the fire. Both jumped up. The dogs jumped up too and began barking.

"Something's roused ol' Buster." Lighting the lantern and going for his boots, Tom said, "I'd better go see."

Jesse grabbed his Winchester-94 from over the fireplace. "I got'cher back. Dicken! Maggie, shutup!"

Jesse opened the door and both dogs disappeared into the darkness. The men moved to the barn. Tom rushed over to try and calm the horse.

"Whoa, Buster. Easy, boy." Tom reassured the horse while Jesse, rifle in one hand and lantern in the other, searched the four corners of the barn.

"Don't see nothin' here. You look to Buster. I'll take a look around outside."

As he left the barn, clouds that had been obscuring the moon, parted. Jesse, deciding he could see better without it, left the lantern near the barn. He stood motionless for a few moments while his eyes adjusted to the moonlight. Everything was black and silver under the moon. He could discern no movement.

The dogs began barking furiously. Clutching his rifle in both hands, Jesse moved off in the direction of the noise.

As quickly as it had begun, the barking stopped. Jesse hesitated. He looked around. He heard nothing beyond his own blood pounding in his ears. Nothing moved other than his breath vaporizing in the cold.

He heard the dogs running toward him now. As they rushed up, silently with tails between their legs, Jesse went down on one knee, checking to see if they were hurt in any way. Both dogs were all right, but curiously subdued. Each tried to get closer to the protection of Jesse's legs.

He stood silently, quieting the dogs' movements and listened. He could see nothing moving. All was silent. Dicken whimpered and huddled closer to Maggie.

"See anything?"

Jesse jumped as Tom stepped up behind him. "Holy shit! Ya nearly scared the piss out'a me!" No, I ain't seen nothing, but these dogs are sure spooked. I am too, truth be told."

"Damn, it's cold," said Tom. "We shoulda brung the whiskey."

Jesse looked toward the house. All appeared normal. Smoke rose from the chimney, inviting them all to return to its warmth.

"You got the lantern?" Jesse asked. Its light no longer shone from near the barn door, where he'd left it.

"No. I thought you had it. Must'a run out of fuel."

Jesse shivered as the moon disappeared behind a cloud. "Let's get inside. Leave the lantern. I'll fetch it in the morning."

The two men and both dogs, all huddling together, made their way in the dark, back to the house. Jesse threw a log on the fire, as much for the light as the heat, and resumed his place. The dogs cowered at his feet, but did not go to sleep. Instead, they kept looking at the door, as if they were waiting for something . . . or someone.

Tom poured them both another whiskey and took a long swallow. Then he sat and relit his pipe.

They were silent for a time. Jesse appeared nervous. He kept looking at the door as if he were expecting someone. Tom noticed that he hadn't replaced his rifle over the fireplace, but kept it close at hand. The flickering light from the fireplace threw dancing shadows on the walls.

A sudden tap – tapping at the door made them both jump. The dogs alerted, but remained close to Jesse. Both men were standing now, looking at the door.

"Wonder who that could be," said Tom. "I'll go see."

"Wait!" Jesse held up his hand. With the other he picked up his rifle.

A minute went by, and then another. The two men stood transfixed. A loud bang on the door made them all jump. Then the door was thrown inward, off its hinges and fell to the floor. Out of the darkness stepped the creature. Its eyes gleamed madly in the light thrown by the fireplace. It stood in the doorway emitting a strange, guttural sound, almost a moaning.

"Oh, my good Lord Jesus!" said Tom, his eyes wide with fright. "What in God's name is that?"

Jess, kept his eyes locked on the creature while bending to retrieve his rifle. Bringing it up to his chest, he worked the lever, sending a round into the chamber as he said, "It's Billy. Billy's come home."

Dicken growled and then sprang toward the creature. Catching the dog like a football, the creature lifted him up over his head and hurled him across the room. Dicken slammed against the wall, fell to the floor and lay inert.

Jesse carefully took aim at the creature's chest. It looked at him for a moment and then, baring it teeth in a snarl, lunged toward him. The rifle's report resonated loudly off the walls.

The creature was thrown back. Clutching its chest it howled in pain. Then it died as it staggered and fell to the floor.

"I knew he'd come home tonight," said Jesse. "It's his mother's birthday."

The Gauntlet

Bangkok. Early 1961. A tall stranger walked the dark streets, carefully avoiding the street lights. To any casual observer who happened to catch him in the light, his height of more than two meters indicated that he was probably Caucasian, possibly European. A wide brimmed fedora shadowed most of his face. His military cut mustache helped mask his features. That, and his long, loosely draped overcoat, lent him an aura of mystery. He stalked through the night with the grace of a cat.

The streets were mostly deserted. It had rained and the wet pavement glistened in the dim light cast by the occasional street lamp. Taxis sped or cruised by at random intervals depending on whether or not they carried a fare.

The tall foreigner stopped in the shadows along a stone wall, behind which resided the Temple of the Emerald Buddha. He looked closely at the two story brick building across the street. It had no markings to indicate its function. There were no windows facing the street. A single, unlit recessed doorway was the only break in an otherwise blank façade.

The man studied the building. He knew the roof was festooned with antennas, though none could be seen from the street. He had learned all about the goings on inside from his personal observation and his contacts in French intelligence. He knew the building was used by the Americans for intelligence operations.

He watched the building every night for a week; each night from a different shadowed location. On two of those nights he followed an individual, apparently the same person, who had exited the building and hurried up the street. The diminutive size of the person indicated it was either a woman, or an Asian man, undoubtedly a Thai national. The object of the tall stranger's interest walked like a man, and wore a long trench coat with a fedora, much like himself. On both occasions the subject kept to the shadows and walked quickly through the streets, frequently changing directions. Often the subject stopped and looked back to ensure he wasn't followed, then hailing a cab, rode to different destinations, exited and entered nearby buildings.

The tall foreigner followed stealthily, waiting several minutes for the subject to emerge, and then followed that person's return to the American intelligence building by roundabout means. Both times he learned the next day of the violent death of someone in a building at the same time the subject of his surveillance had been there.

On a third occasion, the person left the intelligence building and walked speedily as before. This time the stranger closed quickly and silently, on his prey. Closing in on the subject, he pulled from his pocket a garrote about 150 centimeters long and made from double-strand WD-1, military communications wire.

Grasping the ends in each hand, the man crossed his arms at the elbows, raised his arms, and dropped the loop of wire over his victim's head. The tall stranger jerked the loop so violently, he nearly decapitated his victim. He disappeared into the dark, but not before he extracted a Walther PPK pistol from his prey's coat pocket.

The victim lay on the sidewalk, dead.

The tall stranger left the shadows and crossed the street. He walked up the three steps in the dark doorway to a single door, and paused to study the walls on either side. No means of contacting the occupants of the building was evident. Finally he saw a small button close to the door. He pushed it once and waited. He sensed he was being watched, but couldn't detect the location of the watcher.

A voice spoke from somewhere behind the door. "Yes. May I help you?"

"I am here for the position."

While both voices spoke English, it would have been obvious to any listener that this was not their native language.

A light came on. The tall man stood exposed to his questioner.

"Wait here," the voice commanded.

The light went out. The tall man stood patiently in the dark for long moments.

Then the door opened. A Thai man of indeterminate age stood in the doorway. "Follow me," he said.

The tall stranger doffed his fedora as he followed his guide down a dimly lit hall toward a door at its end. On either side they passed by closed doors. The man's footsteps were muffled on the tiled floor. His guide made no noise. He seemed to glide across the tiles.

They stopped before the door at the end of the hall. The guide knocked discreetly, as if afraid of disturbing whoever was inside.

"Come." A muffled voice sounded from beyond the door.

The guide opened the door, stood aside, and invited the tall man to enter. The door shut behind him. He stood in a smallish office before an oversized oaken desk. A Caucasian man sat behind the desk with arms folded, studying him as he looked around. The walls held no decoration. The only other furniture was a scarred straight chair against one wall, and a similar chair placed in front of the desk.

The tall stranger felt too big for his surroundings. He appeared to study them while catching furtive glimpses of his host, a medium sized man with brown hair, parted on the left side. He wore military issue plastic framed bifocals that enlarged his blue eyes, as he stared at his visitor for some minutes.

Finally he unfolded his arms and motioned for the tall man to sit in the chair before him.

Again a period of silence as each of them appeared to be trying to stare the other down.

Finally the man behind the desk said, "Why are you here?" He spoke like an American.

"I came for the position."

"What position?"

"The vacant position."

"We have no vacant position."

"Yes you do." The tall stranger spoke with a slight accent, French possibly or Algerian.

"What is your name?" the American asked as he leaned forward and picked up a *Dixon Ticonderoga*. He began to fidget with the pencil. He was surely an American, from the East Coast, New England probably.

"Claude."

"Claude? Claude what?" The American cocked his head and frowned.

"Claude Lellange. What is your name?"

"Anthony. I am called Tony. Your name sounds French? You look Eurasian."

"My father was French. I was born in Vietnam. My mother was Tonkinese. More recently I resided in Morocco."

"Was your mother from the north?"

"My mother was born and died near Haiphong . . . in the north."

"And your father? What did he do?"

"My father was an officer in the French Army. He died at Dien Bien Phu." Claude raised his head slightly, proudly."

"And you? What is your occupation?"

"Until lately I also was in the French Army, the First Parachute Regiment of the Foreign Legion. I too was at Dien Bien Phu. I watched my father die there. When it was over, I was posted to Algeria with the Legion." Claude started to say more, but suddenly realized he'd said too much. He cast his eyes downward.

The silence lasted some moments.

"And now? What do you do now?"

He has that blunt way of speaking shared by most Americans. "My profession is that of the man I am to replace, only I am much better at it than he . . . was."

Tony's eyes widened. He began to twirl the pencil. "And how do you know that?"

Claude leaned forward and looked sharply at Tony. He started to say something.

Tony dropped the pencil, and held up both his hands. "Never mind. Don't say anything. I believe you."

Claude relaxed and sat back in his chair

Tony continued, changing the subject. "We must do a complete background check. That will take some weeks, maybe months. If you are cleared and you pass a preliminary test, you will be hired on a year's probation. If you are selected, you will be expected to reside in this building. What are your questions?"

"What is this preliminary test?"

Tony reached down and pulled a file folder from a desk drawer.

An Old Soldiers Prayer

I grow old
Nevermore will I challenge the world
Parachute from airplanes
Fight the good fight
Win my war

I grow old
I grow impatient with everyday pains
Muscles failing to work
Children complain
I can't help

I grow old
Little patience with the mundane
I long to face death
Fight the fight
Lose the war

I grow old
Wife understands
Children live on
Death approaches
I wait

PART II: PEACE

Aunt Marian's New Bathroom

In 1942, when I was seven years old, my Uncle Clarence had an indoor bathroom installed as a surprise for my Aunt Marian. Always before, they made use of the old single-seater outhouse, equipped with a Sears and Roebuck catalog doing double duty. During New England winters the call of nature offered, at best, a distasteful chore; at worst, during one of our blizzards, it presented a hellish ordeal.

Uncle Clarence and Aunt Marian Ames were my most favorite of all relatives. Clarence was a truck farmer in Natick, Massachusetts, just a few miles west of Boston. He owned no land of his own, except the lot that contained his house, a homestead his family had owned since revolutionary times.

He rented bits and pieces of pasture land all over Middlesex County. He grew all sorts of fruits and veggies, displaying them for sale each summer, in a roadside produce stand. That is, Aunt Marian would sell the fruit and veggies, for she was the one who minded the store while Clarence hauled the produce.

I said they were my favorites, but really I was referring to my aunt, for Marian was a fantastic cook. She had a hearty laugh, which she shared often, and with the flimsiest of excuses, whereas Uncle Clarence was dour, hardly ever smiled, and kept pretty much to himself.

My dad always accused my uncle of being stingy. He, my uncle that is, never bought anything on credit, but always paid cash. If his family needed something and didn't have the cash for it, then they'd go without. I think my dad was a little jealous of

Clarence because, after all, they did own their own house and we never did.

During the warm New England summers, almost every day Aunt Marian made strawberry shortcake with berries grown by Uncle Clarence, and her salmon loaf was to die for. My mouth watered in anticipation whenever I was told we were to visit them.

Summer of '42, my aunt and uncle invited our whole clan over for Sunday dinner. There was us, the Dixons. There were Grandma and Grandpa Viles, my mom's parents. My Old Maid Aunt Eunice, grumpy as always, because she was too ugly to catch a man (at least that's what my dad claimed) was there, along with my cousin, Eddie, named after Ed Ames the singer and TV star, who wasn't invented yet, because there wasn't any TV. Rounding out this rogue's gallery were our distant cousins, the Dirty Necked Chisholms.

While we were all happy to be invited for dinner, we didn't know that Marian had a surprise for us. When we were all assembled she announced, "Everyone follow me. I have a surprise for you."

As a group we rose and trundled through the back hall to see the surprise, a new indoor bathroom. Of course it was too small to hold everyone at once, so we had to take turns. We all had to try it out, prolonging the procedure *ad nauseum*. And of course everyone had to comment about it.

My mom said, "That's nice." No matter what the event she always responded with her Mona Lisa smile and said, "That's nice."

My dad said, "Always thought he was too cheap to spend the money."

Aunt Eunice said, "Why'd they make me go outside this morning when they knew all along this was here?"

Everybody tried to squeeze in ahead of the Chisholm clan because we knew they'd be in need of baths.

When this was all over, Uncle Clarence announced, "Everybody outside for the marshmallow roast."

Naturally, we kids all hurried outside. Clarence led us all out back to the faded red outhouse.

When we were all gathered, swatting mosquitoes, and looking about for the fire, Uncle Clarence shouted, "Everybody step back!" Then he struck a match and touched it to the outhouse. I guessed it had been primed with kerosene, because it suddenly flared up in a great one-holer bonfire.

As the flames burned down, we broke out the sticks and roasted marshmallows. Funny thing is, nobody but us kids wanted to eat them. There was, as I remember, a distinctly acrid odor in the air.

After a while we went back inside for a grand meal put together by my Aunt Marian, God rest her Protestant soul, but that's another story. Anyhow, that's how my Aunt Marian got her new indoor bathroom.

Justice

When I was eleven years old, I took to the city streets of Boston trying to make some spending money. After school I peddled the Boston American, a daily tabloid, in the bars and on street corners. "Hey! Boston American here!" I'd shout out my wares, announcing the day's headlines, "Read all about it! Back Bay bank robbed by masked bandits! Hey! Boston American here!"

I bought the papers for a penny a copy, and sold them for three cents. Usually, I had enough money to buy twenty or so, enough to last me from when school let out until dark. If I sold them all I'd have close to a buck. With tips, I sometimes made as much as two bucks.

Two bucks was a lot of money in 1946. If I sold papers and made two bucks a day for five days I'd have a sawbuck by the end of the week—a fortune for a kid my age. Of course it never worked out that way.

The newspaper only came out on weekdays. Weekends, I shined shoes for ten cents a shine. I made my own shoe-shine box, and invested coins made from selling papers to buy the brushes and polishes needed to do a first-rate shine job.

I learned to spend my money as fast as I earned it, for to save it was to lose it to one or both of my parents. My mother would borrow my cash for groceries—never to repay. My father would ransack my room for booze money, trying to discover where I hid it this week. If he didn't find it, he'd wait for me to come home, and then knock me around until I told him where it was. Usually I left a small stash where he could find it.

Wandering the streets of Boston, trying to raise a little coin, was not a pastime for the faint-hearted. Especially, if you weighed less than a hundred pounds and were not quite five feet tall. I learned to sense the mood on entering a particular bar. Most of the time they were quiet places for the steady bar flies to drink the afternoons away. Sometimes one or more of them were feeling mean, and looking for a fight. If the bar didn't feel right, I'd pass it by that day. Other bars I avoided all the time.

Whenever I spotted a suit, or a cop I'd get ready to disappear fast. Cops always asked too many questions, or just ran you off. A man wearing a suit was either a wise guy, or a bookie who would take your money as fast as he could shake it out of you.

Shining shoes brought another set of challenges. Making money was more than just a matter of finding a spot in the sun and setting up shop. The best spots, in high traffic areas, were usually taken. The residing shine boy normally wouldn't share unless you were really good buddies. Try to move in on a good spot that was taken and you'd likely wind up with a black eye or a bloody nose and empty pockets.

Some entire neighborhoods were off-limits too. Like the Back Bay. Try to shine shoes there and you'd likely have the Daughters of the American Revolution demanding your arrest as a juvie delinquent.

I'd usually cruise until I found a good corner that was not occupied. I'd hawk the best shine in town for a dime. If business was good I'd get a lot of tips. Saturdays were the best days. Wing-tipped shoes were the best tippers. My usual haul for Saturday was a couple bucks.

If a cop showed up, I'd watch him real close. If he looked at me and scowled I'd beat it. If he smiled at me, I'd offer him a shine—no charge. I'd give him a really good spit shine and he'd, more often than not, spring for a quarter.

My favorite spot to work was located on a corner where there was a bar and a pool hall close by. I'd always try to show up before the corner was taken by another shine boy. This spot was frequented by a lot of potential customers.

One day business was slow, and I was sitting on my shine box, daydreaming, when a pair of heavy, black Brogans walked into my line of sight. I knew a cop had to be attached to those shoes. I looked up, and sure enough there stood a Bluecoat, double row of brass buttons and all. Smiling down at me, he swung his nightstick lazily as he whistled a tune.

"Hey, kid, what's your name?" He asked in a friendly un-policeman sort of way.

I stood and answered defensively, my nerves telling me to prepare for flight. "My name? My name is Joey, Joey Cullin." I looked at the pavement.

"Joey Cullin is it? That's a good Irish name."

His tone of voice told me he was still smiling. I looked up at him. He offered a great thorny hand and said, "Mine's Ahern, Timothy Ahern. I'm pleased to make your acquaintance, Joey."

I couldn't help but smile back at him. It was catching.

He continued, "I think my big flat feet are needing of a shoe-shine. You think you can help me?"

For a minute I just gawked. Then realizing what he said I answered, "sure, Mister . . . ah, Officer Ahern."

After that he came by my corner every Saturday for a shine. He could be counted on for a good tip, especially close to payday. I became accustomed to hearing him whistling an Irish tune to announce his approach. We became friends . . . sorta.

Local wise-guys were usually hanging around pitching pennies or playing

uno-due-trei, the Italian version of rock-scissors-paper, for nickels. Too old to be in school, too young to be bonafide gangsters, one or two of them were always good for a shine. They were lousy tippers, though.

There was this one guy, usually dressed in a light colored, shark-skin, doubled-breasted suit. He wore black wing tips, and while he was usually good for a shine, he always insisted on paying a nickel.

"Hey, kid," he'd say, "how much for a shine?"

"Ten cents, one thin dime for the best shine this side of town."

"Give ya a nickel."

"Uh, uh," I would say, shaking my head vigorously. "Everybody pays a dime and gives a tip if they wanna."

Grabbing me by my shirt and shaking me, he'd say something like, "Why you little jerk! Gimme a nickel's worth or I'll shine my shoes with your shirt, while you're wearin' it."

Grudgingly I would set about giving him a shine. He would whistle through his teeth and smoke a cigarette while I worked.

"All finished," I'd say, hoping he wouldn't notice what a crummy job I'd done.

"Great, my man," he'd say and skipping away from my shine box, flip a nickel toward me. He'd laugh and hurry off down the street like he had someplace to go. I'd walk over and retrieve the nickel, slamming it into my pocket.

I'll get even with you, you big palooka, if it's the last thing I do.

His friends watched the show, snickering among themselves.

Several times over the next few weeks, this wise-guy caught me unawares and insisted I give him a nickel shine. One Saturday I was just finishing one of his shoes when I heard the unmistakable whistling that told me Officer Ahern was coming. I looked up and there he was, night stick swinging around his elbow as he approached, his eyes locked on my wise-guy.

I jumped up. "Officer Ahern!" I called out. "You're just in time. I was just finishing up this customer."

"Whatta ya mean, finishing up?" said the wise-guy. "You still got one shoe to go!"

"I don't think so. I think you're all finished now." I took a step backward as he reached for me.

"Hold it right there, Punk!" said Officer Ahern. He stepped up and poked the wise-guy in the stomach with his night stick. "I'm looking at these shoes and I don't believe I ever seen a more perfect shine. No sir, this is as good as it gets."

The wise-guy looked down at his shoes; one shiny, the other dirty. Then he looked up at Officer Ahern and swallowed.

"As a matter of fact," Ahern poked him again with his stick. "I think this job is worth far more than a dime, don't you?" Another poke and the punk's back was up against the building. His buddies watched from the corner of their eyes while they pretended to be absorbed in a game of uno-duo-trei.

"Yeah, yeah, sure. I'll spring for two bits."

"Two bits! Why this job is easily worth a buck!" said Ahern. "Or do we need to go down to the station and discuss it with the desk sergeant?"

"Naw, here's a buck." The punk reached into his pocket, and pulled out a dollar bill. He threw it toward me. It fell to the ground.

"Pick it up!" Ahern ordered. The punk hesitated for a moment, watching his friends watching him. "I hope you're not going to piss me off," said Ahern. "When I get pissed I get mean." He twirled his night stick menacingly.

Wincing, the wise-guy quickly picked up the dollar bill.

"Now, hand it to the boy nicely and thank him for the shine." The wise-guy hesitated. "Do it!"

"Thanks for the shine, kid. Be seein' ya," the wise-guy Said, looking at me through slitted eyes. I knew I was in big trouble if he ever got me alone.

"That's better," said Officer Ahern. "Now let me give you a piece of advice. I patrol this beat every Saturday. I better not ever see you on it again. If I do, I'll run you in and decide later what the charge is. Get it!" He poked the punk once more with the stick.

"Yeah, yeah! I get it!"

"Good, now get lost. And take your friends with you. Now!"

The three wise-guys beat it down the street. Officer Ahern turned to me and put a hand on my shoulder. "Better lay low for a while Joey. I'll keep my eyes open, but you stay out of way of those punks from now on."

Several days later, after school I picked up some papers and, walking down the street, began my usual pitch. "Hey! Boston America here! Read all about it! Local patrolman gunned down in pool hall gun bat . . . tle . . . .

I stopped and looked at the front page. There was a picture of Officer Ahern. I read the article through tears. I couldn't believe it. The officer had been ambushed by thugs hiding in the pool hall. They shot him five times. He'd managed to defend himself, and killed two of the men before succumbing to his wounds. Pictures of the dead men were on the second page. One of them was my nickel customer.

I dropped the papers to the sidewalk and ran home, tears streaming from my face. I blamed myself for Officer Ahern's death. He was only trying to help me. Where was the justice in his death?

To this day, whenever I see a cop walking a beat, I can close my eyes and hear Officer Ahern whistling an Irish tune, and swinging his nightstick. He taught me that policemen are my friends. Somewhere along the jagged line toward manhood when I first heard it said, "Justice is blind," I knew exactly what that meant.

Jamboree

When I was fifteen I feared life was going to pass me by. I was growing older by the hour and felt I had experienced little in the way of adventure. In my callowness I believed that one could only experience the adventures of life through travel to exotic foreign lands, like Florida. My traveling had been confined to the New England states. I lived for a brief time in New York State, but at the time I was only four years old and remembered little of it. The world as I had seen it had thus far consisted of green leaves in summer and snow in winter.

In my junior year of high school, I learned one day that a friend's family was planning to move to New Mexico at the end of the school year. I saw New Mexico in my imagination as an exotic place of deserts filled with Indians dressed in leathers and feathers. In my mind's eye I could see miles of wide open spaces with snow-capped mountains in the distance. How I envied my friend his good fortune. I despaired of ever seeing anything beyond the back alleys of the South End of Boston.

In my senior year, I was told my Scout Troop had selected me to go to The Netherlands to attend a jamboree. Our troop sponsors, The Salvation Army, would pay my way. This jamboree was to be for all scouts everywhere sponsored by "The Sally" and would be the first international Boy Scout jamboree to be held in Europe since the onset of World War II.

Huzza! My adventure was to happen after all. The adventure of my life was about to begin. Holland qualified as an exotic place. I wouldn't grow old never having left New England.

Scouts and Scouting leaders from different parts of the Eastern United States, seventeen of us, gathered at a summer camp in New Jersey. We spent a week getting to know one another and building our American team before embarking across the Atlantic for Europe. Our assigned leader was a scoutmaster from the Bronx. We were invited to call him "Scottie."

The next week we went to Hoboken where we boarded a ship for Rotterdam. From Rotterdam we were bussed to the small town of Ede, close to the Rhine River and Arnhem.

Much later I was to learn the history of this part of Europe via stories like "A Bridge Too Far."

Arriving in camp we learned that we were the first "foreign" contingent to arrive. It was the first, but not the last time I was to hear myself referred to as a foreigner. We and a group of local Dutch Scouts were expected to set up the entire camp in preparation for the arrival Scouts from more than a dozen European countries. This sounded like a big job until we learned that 150 English scouts were to arrive the next day. Their arrival multiplied our work force exponentially. They were led by a robust pirate of a man called Skipper Davies by all the Brit scouts. Together with the English and the Dutch we set about establishing the "Motondo" campsight in an open field. I never did learn what Motondo meant, but it sounded exotic. It rained almost every day we were in camp.

As our days as freely indentured pioneer laborers in The Netherlands passed, I learned some things about the Dutch. Though it was 1952, the war had been over for more than six years, they still despised the Germans because of the occupation during the war and held little love for the English because Royal Air Force bombs had destroyed many of their cities. I remembered seeing damaged buildings extant in Rotterdam.

We had to adjust to the local diet. Meat was scarce; the most commonly offered being a canned "liver paste" served up in cans like our potted meat. I had never liked the taste of liver, but came to crave it. A staple in Holland seemed to be bread with jam and tea. The bread was very substantive and we learned to make do, for the greatest part of our diet, with bread and jam.

In the cities and towns, we learned a favorite snack-cum-lunch was whole, pickled herring vended from itinerant fifty-gallon glass jars carried on bicycle-driven wagons. Hollanders relished these herring and swallowed them whole. As much as I tried I couldn't down the "whole thing," but have since learned to enjoy pickled herring in bite sized portions as preferred by American Scandinavians.

During one of our days off, we Americans brought out a softball and bat and began a pickup game in an open field. Several English scouts stopped to watch us and soon they wanted to play. We whipped them handily and when the game was finished they challenged us to a football game to be played the following day.

"Okay! Football! That's our game. But we don't have a football."

"That's okay, blokes. We'll bring one. Meet you here at tennish, right?"

The next day we showed up to play and the English showed us their football. It was a soccer ball. One American scout said, "What are we supposed to do with that undersized basketball?"

We had never seen, nor even heard of soccer, but this was what the English called "football."

"That's okay, mates. We'll show you how we play football, just like you showed us how to play your American baseball."

We were soundly whipped and wore the bruises of that demonstration of soccer for several days.

I needed a haircut and went into the village of Ede to see if I could find a barber shop. It was my first visit to a Dutch farming village and the first time I'd been able to get away on my own hook in Holland. I walked down the single main street gawking at the things offered for sale. The people were more interesting. All wore wooden shoes. Their steps made a constant cacophony of noise on the cobbles of the single street.

I identified the barber shop by its ubiquitous red and white striped pole. There were two pairs of wooden shoes placed in tandem beside the entrance, so I removed my U.S. Keds sneakers, placed them beside the wooden shoes, and walked in. The shop looked much like one of ours; one chair dominated the single-roomed shop. Hair-cutting tools and lotions covered a shelf beneath a large mirror. Two townies were engaged in, I supposed, the usual gossip with the barber. Now he turned his attention to me and said something. Of course it was in Dutch.

I didn't speak Dutch, but two years of high school German gave me a rudimentary understanding of this guttural Germanic tongue. I answered in English rather than German because I'd been told that while the Dutch understood German, they didn't especially appreciate hearing the language. There were two things of which they were particularly fond: Americans and Boy Scouts. They loved their Scouts, called "Potfinders" in Dutch. They were extremely proud of the role their potfinders had played as members of the Dutch Resistance, or Underground during WWII. They recognized Americans as

149

having liberated them from the Nazis. They held us in the same regard as their own scouts.

By supplementing my request with hand signs, the barber understood me and motioned me toward the chair. I watched his face in the mirror as he covered my chest with a white sheet and continued talking to his two cronies, while brandishing a straight razor before my face. I understood that he was telling his friends that I was English. The looks that passed between them told me that none of them were too happy about that. I spoke up loudly, "Nay, Nay. Ich bin Englander nicht. Ich bin Americanse Potfinder."

Despite my poor attempt and my mixed Dutch and German, They understood me, for the transformation was immediate. Now they were all smiles and all talking at once.

The barber went to a back room and returned with a woman who, I learned, was his wife. She spoke passable English. She began to cut my hair while she questioned me non-stop about America. The three men sat listening silently whilst she interpreted my answers to her questions and reported them to all.

When she had finished she invited me to remain for some bread and jam and tea. I tried to pay and go, but they wouldn't let me pay and insisted that I stay and visit. They wanted to hear more about America.

Boy Scout contingents from various European countries in varying numbers continued to arrive in camp. Among them were five German adults who had been Scouts before Hitler's ascendancy, during which time they had been drafted into the Hitlerjugend. They were attempting to rebuild the Scouting

Program in their homeland. They were fine fellows and we all gave them the respect due adult Scout leaders.

One night, sometime after we had all turned in, Scottie came round and awakened us.

"Everyone up. There may be trouble brewing. Get dressed and gather at my tent."

When we had accounted for all seventeen of us, Scottie said simply, "I've been told that some of the local farmers are unhappy that Germany is represented here. We're going over to the German camp to make sure everything's okay. Everybody got your shoes on?" He looked about. Then he nodded his head and said, "Okay. Follow me."

We picked our way through the moonless night to the front entrance of the German camp. Because we'd set it up, it wasn't hard to find our way.

Reaching the German encampment, Scottie said, "You wait here and keep your eyes peeled while I go talk to the Germans."

We waited, but not for long as torches and the sounds of a lot of people approaching, alarmed us. By the light of the torches we could see that a group of farmers had gathered. There must have been at least fifty men and women. Some were armed with pitchforks. They were upset and looking mean. I was reminded of a scene from the movie "Frankenstein," where the farmers have gathered at a windmill, or some such place, to destroy the Monster.

Scottie returned and stood at our front. He Shouted to be heard, "Stop! Halt! Halten sie! What is it you want? Was is los?"

It suddenly got very quiet. We could hear the torches sputtering in the light wind. A voice from the middle of the

151

now silent group said in broken English, "Ve vant the demned Nazis!"

"There are no Nazis here! Only Potfinders," Scottie called out.

"Deutchlanders hide among you! Ve vant dem! Ve are coming through!"

Just then the encampment lit up behind us. Illuminated by flashlight and by lantern stood all 150 of the English contingent arrayed two by two across our rear.

Skipper Davies stepped up beside us and said so all could hear, "I've got 150 British Scouts here who say that if you want the Deutchlanders, you'll have to come through us and the Americans! I tell you as an officer in her Majesty's British Army and the leader of these young men, there are no Nazis in this camp!"

After a long moment of silence the farmers melted away in the dark.

Settling back down into my sleeping bag, I thought to myself, *Holy Moley! Just one week in Europe and I've had all this excitement. I think I'm going to have an exciting life in exotic places after all."*

Jack

It was sunup when Mick saddled Old Buster and headed for the hills. Jack, a black Labrador retriever mix, accompanied him. The stray had been his constant companion ever since Mick's arrival early that summer in Billings. They worked together through Mick's apprenticeship at ranching on the Bailey Ranch, several miles north of Billings. When he applied for work, he could provide no credentials in riding, roping, or anything else of any use around the ranch.

Ned Bailey had been about to turn him away when he spotted Jack. The dog's obvious love for the boy hit a cord in Ned's heart. *Any man, who can win a dog's love, must have something of value within himself.*

As he stood studying the young man standing before him, Ned was impressed by his mien, if not by his size, which was small compared to most Montana cow hands.

"Where you from, boy?" asked Ned.

"I'm not a boy. I'm nearly twenty," responded Mick. "I came to Billings from Boston to become a cowboy. My name is Francis McPherson. I was named after my father, but I think 'Francis' sounds a bit . . . soft, so I ask my friends to call me "Mick.'"

Ned studied him. There was nothing physically to recommend him. He was of less than average height, dark hair and eyes, fair build. Ned looked again at the eyes. There was something there that told him he could be trusted. Ned sensed that crossing the young man would be a mistake.

He said, "We don't run a school here. We run cattle. What do you know about cattle?"

153

"Very little Sir, But I'm a hard worker and a fast learner. I'm an Eagle Scout, if that helps."

"Sure does! Never was a scout myself, but I never met one I couldn't trust. Alright, I'll take you on. You'll catch a lot of ribbing from my ranch hands, but if you're willing to work hard and you catch on fast, you'll do okay. Pay's five dollars a day and found. The dog's included. Let's shake on it, Mick." Ned extended a horny calloused hand.

Ned Bailey wasn't sorry. Mick kept his promise and labored hard at this toughest of work. The ranch hands did ride him whenever he made a mistake, which was often. They kidded him about his Boston twang as well, and referred to him as the "Kid."

After a while the kidding subsided. He worked hard to befriend them all, toiling alongside the best of them from sunup until supper and working until dark on roping and tack-work. Mick was quick to see his own shortcomings and fix them.

One evening, in his third week on the job, he said to Rudy, the closest of his new-found friends, "I think I'll take a ride up into those hills to the north this weekend. Will you help me get ready?"

"Why sure, but what do you want to do that for? Me, at the end of the week all I want to do is take a soak in a horse trough, and ride to town for a beer. Maybe look at some girls."

"Ever since I've been here I've looked at those hills and wanted to go there. Besides I can use the practice at riding."

"Okay, Partner, if you're up to being miserable instead of comfortable, all I can do is help. "Now, those hills are a lot farther away than they look. You're about to find out why they call Montana 'Big Sky Country.' Better plan to spend the weekend. That means sleepin' out. Shit on a shingle, that don't sound like much fun." Rudy finished coiling his lariat and threw it over his saddle horn. "Better ride Old Buster. He's slow, but he's tough, and he's been on roundup, so he knows the scrub.

"There's no water between here and there, so you better carry enough for yourself and a little for your horse. If Jack tags along, and you know he will, you'll need extra water for him too." Rudy scratched his head. "Shit all. Better pull a water wagon. Naw, just kiddin' but you better be careful with the water. No matter how hot it gets, don't take off your Stetson or your shirt. It gets cold at night, so you'll need a blanket."

"That's good advice," said Mick.

"Be sure to take a rope in case Old Buster gets away from you. If he gets nervous you might not be able to walk up on him.

"Can't advise you about food, 'cept be frugal and don't plan on a banquet. Jack won't need to eat. He's all skin and bones anyway. And Buster needs only a little oats. Maybe you'll find some sweet-grass."

"I can go without food. Maybe Cook will give me some jerky. Whatever I take with me, the dog gets half."

"Sure, whatever. You got a hog-leg?

"What's a hog-leg?"

"A six-shooter. There's bears and cougar and snakes. Somebody said he heard a wolf the other night, though I misdoubt his veracity."

"No, I don't own a gun."

"S'okay. I'll lend you mine. Just so's you clean it if you use it. Don't forget your knife and fire fixin's."

155

The air was cool as Mick headed out. Buster's head was up, and he wanted to canter. The young man held him back. Jack trotted alongside, tongue lolling. He looked happy to be included in this adventure.

The sun rose higher in the sky, warming up the prairie. Mick doffed his denim jacket, rolled it with his blanket, and strapped it, behind the saddle.

Looking back, he could barely make out the ranch. Looking ahead, the mountain, his destination, looked to be no closer.

Toward noon it grew hot. Mick stopped, and dismounted to give Jack a drink from his cupped hands. The dog lapped up the water.

As the afternoon shadows lengthened, and the hottest part of the day was over, Mick opined that he had made progress on the mountain. The trio had definitely gained altitude. The ranch was no longer visible in the heat waves rising from the high prairie. Grass had given way to sand and sagebrush. What few trees there were appeared stunted. Rock outcroppings appeared in increasing numbers.

Mick stopped in the shade of one large outcropping. Sitting in the saddle, he took a swig from his canteen. He was just about to dismount and stretch his legs, when Buster shied and whinnied. Before Mick could quiet him, the horse reared and dumped him like a sack of potatoes in the dust. The horse danced away. Buster stopped, and stood shaking his mane, nervously eyeing Mick.

Dazed, Mick lay on his back. He shook his head to clear it, and started to get up. He froze when he heard a spine chilling sound, like pebbles rattling in a gourd. He'd never heard it before, but immediately recognized it as a rattlesnake's warning.

Mick's head spun. He looked toward his feet, splayed somewhere in the dust beyond his nether parts. As his vision cleared, easily discernible within range of his boots, was the biggest Diamondback rattler Mick had ever seen. The fact that it was the only Diamondback he had ever seen didn't stop him from thinking momentarily, *if I see a thousand Diamondback rattlers, this has got to be the biggest.*

Mick began to sweat. The snake was coiled tightly, ready to strike. Its rattle, noisy as a baby's toy, warned of its potency as its tail quivered above its body. Its tongue flicked nervously. Its body was easily six inches thick. Its beady eyes, forward of and below the coil, looked up at the cowboy.

Now I know what they mean by the term 'pit viper'. This whole scene gives new meaning to the term 'the world stood still.'

He wanted to wipe the sweat from his eyes, but didn't dare move.

Buster was restive and Mick tried to calm him. He said, "Whoa, Old Buster. Easy boy. Easy . . ."

Suddenly he thought *where is Jack?* He moved slightly, trying to locate the dog.

The snake struck.

He felt the impact of the serpent's head against the thick sole of his boot. He thought, *Thank God for these heavy work-boots.* He felt, more than, saw the skinny black dog launching itself at the snake. Growling and moving almost as swiftly as the snake struck, Jack lunged, and grabbed the rattler behind its head before it could gather itself for another strike. The dog shook the snake vigorously, whipping it about him.

Mick drew his pistol and held it in both hands as he tried to get a bead on the snake. He was afraid of hitting Jack.

157

Jack gave a sharp yelp and dropped the snake as it sank its fangs into his shoulder. Mick fired twice at the now writhing snake. Both shots missed. Jack staggered and fell prostrate. The snake recoiled, moving more slowly now. Mick took careful aim at the viper's head and fired once more. This time he hit his target, blowing most of the rattler's head away.

Kneeling beside the dog, Mick searched for fang marks. Brushing back the black fur, he spotted two puncture wounds.

Jack lay whimpering and gasping.

The sun disappeared behind mountains. Mick tried to collect himself. He reloaded the pistol and replaced it in its holster. He thought back to his Scout first aid training for snake bite. Holding Jack's head in his lap, Mick stroked his hair and said through tears, "Jack. Jack, boy, its okay. You're going to be alright, boy. You saved my life."

He removed his boot and saw that the sole was covered with venom. "Ah, good. The snake spent most of its venom on the first strike."

At the word "snake," Jack managed a weak, but menacing growl.

Mick drew his knife. "It's okay, boy. I'm going to shave your hair around the bite." He spit on the fur to serve as a lubricant, making it easier to shave a bald spot on Jack's shoulder. Mick could see that there was pronounced swelling now. "I'm going to have to cut you on the fang marks, boy. This won't hurt much . . . I hope."

He sliced once on each mark, causing the dog to bleed freely. Jack was unconscious now and didn't react to the cutting. Without hesitation, feeling the need for haste, Mick began to suck on each fang mark. When he thought he had drawn and spit out most of the venom, he removed the bandana

158

from around his neck, and placed it over the wounds in an attempt to stem the flow of blood. He sat back trying to remember what he should do next.

"Ah, I have an idea, Jack. I remember reading about how the Indians placed a poultice over wounds to draw out poison. I don't suppose there're any good shrubs around here, but I'll use whatever I find."

He sat beside Jack, holding the bandanna in place, stroking the dog's coat and talking to him, until the bleeding stopped. Then he rose to his feet and went to Buster, who stood patiently a few feet away. Stroking the horse's neck, Mick spoke softly to him, "Ol' Buster. You're a good and faithful friend. You gotta help me save Jack."

He retrieved his blanket from behind the saddle, unrolled it, spread it on the ground, and placed Jack on it. He was amazed at how little the dog weighed. He ran his fingers over the dog's ribs.

"Aw, Jack. I need to feed you more and fatten you up a bit. But right now I think I'm gonna be glad you don't weigh much."

Mick made Jack as comfortable as possible on the blanket. Then he went in search of some promising looking leaves with which to make a poultice. He soon returned with a few branches of sage. He knelt once more beside Jack.

Eyes closed and with labored breath, the dog lay unmoving. Mick felt his nose. It was dry and hot.

"Alright, old friend, I'm going to crush these leaves and mix them with mud."

He made some mud with water he could ill afford. Then he mixed in the leaves. When he had a good looking paste, he spread it carefully on Jack's shoulder. The dog whimpered faintly.

"What can I use to hold this in place," Mick thought out loud. "Ah, I know. A snake skin will do nicely."

He quickly skinned out the now dead rattler. "Man, that's a lot of hide. Make a nice belt and maybe a collar for you too, Jack."

When he had the snake skin as clean as he could get it, he wrapped it around the dog's shoulder and neck to hold the poultice in place to keep the wound damp and draining.

"Jack, I don't know if that's going to do any good, but it can't do bad. I hope it'll keep you alive 'til we get home."

Darkness fell as he wrapped the blanket around the dog and held him in his arms, talking to him through the night. He recited every prayer he could remember from his catechism, beginning with "Hail Mary, full of grace . . ." When he had finished with the Our Father, he began again.

Toward morning, Jack woke long enough to lick Mick's face with a tongue that had little moisture in it. Mick moistened his bandana and held it to the dog's nose. Jack opened his eyes momentarily and looked up at Mick, whose eyes teared. "Aw, Jack my best dog, my brother. Please don't die."

In the morning chill, Mick stood to stretch his legs. He was grateful to see Buster was still there, standing quietly, where he had throughout the night.

"Well, Ol' Buster," said Mick as he moved to stroke the horse gratefully, "We gotta find a way to get Jack back to the ranch. This dog saved my life and I will save his."

Mick returned to the dog. Jack was breathing better now. He was still unconscious, but Mick found his nose was cooler.

"That is a good sign. Now, I have to get you up on the horse and back to the ranch." He talked to Jack as he made his plan.

"I know how to do this, if you'll just bear with me, my friend." Mick led the horse over beside the dog. "I'm going to make a cradle with the rope," he continued to talk as he worked. "Now we'll put this rope around you as comfortably as we can."

Mick mounted the horse holding onto both ends of the makeshift cradle holding Jack. "Now I'm going to lift you as carefully as I can." He lifted the dog up and into his arms.

Holding Jack closely to his chest, he wrapped the rope around his own shoulders and supported the dog with his body. Buster looked back at him and remained stationary.

"Alright, old horse, let's go slow."

Mick chucked with his lips and nudged Buster with his heels. The horse began to walk.

As one, the three moved over the prairie toward home.

Mick held the dog in his arms throughout the day as he trusted the horse to carry them back to the ranch.

In the hottest part of the day, Mick was feeling the weight of the dog. He needed badly to stretch his legs, but couldn't let go of his precious cargo. Jack's labored breathing told Mick that he still lived. With his right hand he felt of Jack's nose. It was warm and dry. He poured the last of his water over the dog's face and nose. Jack stirred and whimpering softly, he strecthed and licked Mick's face.

"We're gonna make it, old dog," Mick managed through cracked lips. He hoped Buster would keep going.

There was no more water.

The horse plodded on.

Toward sundown, the wranglers watered their horses and stripped to clean up for supper using the same watering trough, Rudy shouted out, "Yonder comes Old Buster. The kid's aboard and he's carrying some sorta bundle. Looks like a baby."

Buster, head hanging low, plodded through the front gate and stopped at the water trough where he drank. Mick remained in the saddle, cradling Jack. He sat silently. He wondered why the horse had stopped. He licked his dry lips. His mouth was dry.

Rudy ran up to him. "Mick, you okay?"

"Help Jack," Mick mumbled through cracked lips. "He's snake bit."

"help! Get help!" Rudy reached up and untied the rope securing the bundle to Mick.

"The dog needs help! He's been snake bit!" Rudy shouted. "Somebody get Vince!"

Vince was the cowhand who filled in when a veterinarian was needed. He had a special talent with animals. The nearest vet was two days away in Billings.

The ranch hands gathered and helped Mick down from the saddle. They splashed water over Mick and Jack. Rudy held the blanket and its dog.

Buster drank his fill from the trough.

Ned Bailey appeared. "Calm down everybody! Let's see what's going on here. Mick, you okay?"

Mick drank water and coughed, "Look to the dog. He saved my life. He's snake bitten."

162

Later, when Vince had seen to jack and was sure he was out of danger, he went to the ranch house where Mick was resting comfortably in a spare room.

"Dang," said Vince looking around the room, "This here's almost worth wrassling a rattler over. Kid, yer dog's gonna be fine. He's had a rough time of it, but he's restin' in the bunkhouse now. I never saw the like of what you did with that snakeskin, but it worked."

Days later as Mick sat with Ned on the ranch house porch, Jack by his side, Ned Bailey said, "Mick, you've proven yourself to be a real buckaroo. You're welcome to stay at the Bailey ranch for as long as you want. And you have a dollar raise in wages if your dog stays on."

Tahoma Challenge

In the summer of 1956 I was invited to climb Mount Rainier with a party led by a member of our Boeing Ski Club. Bill Chalmers was an aeronautical engineer and an accomplished climber.

Bill had climbed the mountain three times before and he wanted to take the most direct route—the the Kautz Glacier on the northwest side of the mountain with a party of six in mid-July. The party was to be comprised of Bill, Joe Galbraith who was an expert skier but with whose climbing record I was unfamiliar, Walt Daniels an experienced rock climber from California who had never climbed on ice, and a pair of twin brothers the Dahlgrens, Bob and Jimmie big strapping fellows from Pennsylvania. I could never distinguish one twin from the other.

I spent the spring training for the climb on Snoqualmie Pass day climbs and breaking in a new pair of boots.

The morning of the climb dawned clear and sunny—a rare day in Western Washington—not a cloud in the sky. Our party met at the *Poodle Dog* restaurant in Fife for introductions and steak 'n eggs for breakfast.

We formed a caravan of two cars, Bill leading with his pals the Pennsylvania twins, me following in my old '47 Ford with Joe and Walt riding shotgun. We left highway 99 in Tacoma (this was pre I-5) and headed up the mountain to *Paradise* where we would leave the cars for the two-day climb.

We laid our equipment out in the parking lot so the ranger could check us out and assure himself we were properly prepared. We had to wait because another party was ahead of us. Jim Whitaker and a party of three were about to mount an assault for speed in preparation for climbing Mount McKinley.

I had taken climbing lessons from Whitaker, who later was the first American up Everest. I knew him as well as anyone could—he was a moody sort, again my opinion. I approached him and asked him which route he planned to take.

"Well, the doctor here, who's sponsoring our climb of McKinley, trying for a world record time, hasn't much experience. We plan to go the 'tourist' route via Camp Muir and Liberty Ridge. If all goes as planned, we'll be up and back down by noon."

"Well, good luck, Jim. We're going the Kautz route."

Jim turned away without another word as was his way and I returned to my party. "Well they won't be in our way. Matter of fact if their plans work out, they'll be off the mountain before we make first night's camp."

Our plan was to head straight up from Paradise and cross the Nisqually Glacier at about 8,000 feet. From there we'd work our way upward on the lower Kautz Glacier and camp at about 11,500 feet, just below the Kautz Ice Fall.

Next morning we were to ascend the Kautz Ice Fall and climb the upper Kautz glacier to the saddle amid the triple craters of Rainier. From there it was an easy walk to the lip of the remaining crater and the peak along its east side.

The ranger finished his inspection of our gear and began questioning us about our experience. Bill told of his two previous climbs of Rainier and his experience on similar mountains in the northwest. Joe admitted he didn't have much experience above 12,000 feet but he'd been on the Stevens Pass ski patrol for six years. Walt rattled off the many peaks he'd climbed in California as did the Dahlgren twins about their

165

exploits in the Northeast. I explained my training with the Washington Alpine Club and we were cleared to go. As we donned our gear and packs I noticed the Dahlgren twins were carrying extra gear on pack-boards. I couldn't carry that much even if I wanted to. They were built like Neanderthals and I opined they were up to the task.

We started up at about 0930. The sun hadn't risen on our side of the mountain, but the sky was a deep azure. The snow was crusted and easy to walk on. We left half-inch foot prints as we worked our way up from 6,000 feet.

Soon the sun came 'round the mountain and we stopped to apply clown white as a sunburn deterrent. Bill said, "I think we better put on our snow goggles and this is a good place to rope up and put on our crampons. We'll soon be crossing the Nisqually Glacier. If conditions are right, I want to practice some crevasse extraction there."

We worked our way upward on three-man ropes. I stumbled a bit as I accustomed myself to wearing the crampons. The others did as well. Our breathing became labored. We were all accustomed to living at sea level.

We reached the Nisqually Glacier around noon and stopped for lunch. We sat roped up in the snow, chewing on nut bars. I carried a jar of stuffed olives as was my custom. I always developed a craving for stuffed olives when I climbed. Perhaps it was for the salt and the fat. Anyway I ate the whole thing and placed the empty jar in my backpack. In those days we were careful to maintain the pristine cleanliness of the Cascade wilderness.

After lunch we re-applied the clown white because the sun was full on us now. We trudged up and across the glacier switch-backing around the ends of the cobalt blue openings in the ice until Bill stopped us beside one wide-open crevasse.

"This looks like a prime crevasse," Bill said. "The bottom is visible only about thirty feet down. We'll set up on the uphill side and take turns dropping into the crevasse. The object is to self-extract as much as we can. The others will practice belays and setting up for the extraction."

We took a breather in the sunshine. The reflected heat from the ice had us sweating. We gathered on the lip of the crevasse. I looked down into cobalt blue nothingness.

"Who's first," Bill said.

"I'll go," I said and stepped forward. I'd taken training the previous summer in crevasse extraction on this very glacier.

"Okay, Dick will rapelle down into the mouth of the crevasse. I will set up a belay at the lip. Joe will back me up with a belay at the end of his rope. Once we have Dick stable at the end of the rope and we have determined that he is not injured, he will begin to work his way up, using his prussic slings. Once we have him to the lip, the lead man on the second rope will assist him to exit the crevasse. You got that?"

I checked my climbing rope and prussic slings. We carried two half-inch nylon climbing ropes. Each of them was one hundred and twenty feet long. We roped in at sixty foot intervals, three to a rope. Additionally we were each equipped with three prussic slings of one quarter inch thick nylon. Each sling was, looped and tied in a square knot backed by overhand knots.

The prussic slings were secured to the climbing rope, one tied in a prussic knot (sort of like a double girth hitch. It was a knot tied to the main climbing rope that could be moved freely in either direction on the rope but would bind when pulled on from an angle.) The first prussic sling was looped around each shoulder to form a support. The other two slings were used to slide up the rope and step upward in extraction.

I stepped over the edge of the crevasse and dropped down. I let myself slide into the increasing cold. Immediately, I began to shiver. The temperature dropped at least twenty degrees.

I heard Bill's voice from above. "Belay on. Dick, begin to climb."

I placed my foot into one prussic sling and prayed I'd tied the knots correctly. The sling held and I stepped upward in its stirrup about a foot. I slid the other sling upward as far as I could reach. Then I stepped up with the other foot.

The third sling was looped around my chest and under my armpits. I slipped the knot upward until it was taught. Then I began the laborious drill again. I repeated these steps until my head was above the rim of the crevasse. Immediately I felt warmer. My extremities were beginning to lose feeling.

"This is the critical spot," Bill said as he held me head and shoulders above the edge of the crevasse. "We have to get another sling over his head and under his arms in order to pull him out. Otherwise he might freeze to death in place. I've seen it happen."

Each man took his turn in the crevasse and working his way upward using the slings. In later years, the development of the *Jumar Ascender* would make the task of climbing out of a crevasse a lot easier.

We worked our way across the Nisqually Glacier and onto the lower Kautz Glacier. The air got thinner. The going was slow as we plodded on, wearing our crampons, one step at a time. Each of us fell into a "rest-step" cadence. Each step was

168

hard work. Between the efforts to take each uphill stride we'd relax momentarily, and then step forward.

Sundown found us high on the mountain and on a gravel moraine protruding out of the glacial ice.

"We'll bivouac here until daylight." Bill said. We were at about 12,500 feet. Breathing, by this time had become our primary task. The Kautz Ice Fall stood brooding over us, a broken wall of ice looking like a waterfall suddenly frozen in time. It was a daunting sight in the fading daylight.

We looked for spaces among the boulders to pitch two-man pup tents. Wire pegs weighted down with two-man rocks kept them erect in the gravelly soil between the boulders. We carried three tents. Bill and Joe camped together. The Philly twins camped together. Walt was stuck with me, or I was stuck with Walt, Whichever way you wanted to look at it. Anyway, neither of us snored. That was a good thing.

We tried to cook some rations. The water boiled while it was still cold. Walt tried some beans, but they were dried out before they were hot enough to eat. I decided to make do with my last jar of stuffed olives and an orange. Walt settled for some *Gorp* made from raisins and nuts and whatever.

We spent the night listening to boulders come barreling down the mountain. The ground shook as they ricocheted from rock to rock. Their booming kept us on edge all night. We shrank into our sleeping bags praying that the rocks would miss us.

Dawn broke late on the Western side of the mountain. In half light I was up and heating some tea on my alcohol stove as best as I could. Walt was up and packing his gear. I offered him some luke-warm tea. He accepted it gratefully.

Bill and Joe began to pack their tent and gear.

The Philly twins' tent remained silent. "I better go roust 'em out," Bill said.

A few minutes later, Bill emerged from the tent alone. "Bob's got altitude sickness. Jimmie elects to stay back with him until we return. Better saddle up."

The four of us started for the top in the pre-dawn cold. Soon we left the graveled ridge and roped up, two to a rope. Doubled, the rope allowed sixty feet between climbers and provided a softer cushion should anyone fall. We encountered glacial ice and donned our crampons.

We reached the foot of the ice fall when Bill called a halt. "Joe has fallen ill and says he can't continue. I'll take him back down to the basecamp. Dick, you and Walt continue on. We'll be waiting for you."

"But, Bill," I said. "You're the most experienced climber and this is your show. One of us should stay back."

I was thinking about Walt's lack of experience on snow and ice. My thought was that Walt would stay back while Bill and I continued on. I didn't like the look of that ice fall.

"I've been up the mountain several times. You and Walt should have your chance. It'll be alright."

We watched Bill and Joe descend. "Well, Walt, 'and then there were two Indians left.' Should we quit, too, or do you feel like continuing?"

"You're the leader now. I want to go on. We only have about 1,500 left to the top. I've never been this high with my feet still on the ground."

"All right. If you're game, so am I. Let's make like shepherds and get the flock out of town."

It was much colder here on the face of the ice fall. I looked upward at the sheet ice draped across the vertical expanse.

1500 feet to go—it might as well be a mile.

The cold was welcome—it kept the footing from being slippery. Working our way up the often vertical face, we were surprised to learn that it was formed of rippled ice flows running almost horizontal. It seemed like we were climbing Paul Bunyan's wash board.

We kept the doubled rope taut between us as we climbed. I kept an eye on Walt, sixty feet behind me. He looked strong, following my steps precisely.

It took about two hours to reach the top of the ice fall. We rested in the rising warmth of the sun just peeking over the top of the mountain. Above, the glacier spread like a giant white football field slanted at a forty-five degree angle. Criss-crossing the glacier like cerulean tiger stripes were the openings of countless crevasses.

"Wow," Walt said. "I've never seen anything as beautiful or as humongous as this. I suppose those blue streaks mark the upper lips of crevasses."

"Indeed they do. We can see them going up, but coming down they won't be evident. We should have brought the glacier wands to mark our trail, but Bill has them all."

The sun appeared over the peak. We donned our goggles and worked our way, rest-stepping into the ever-higher altitude, switch-backing amid the seemingly bottomless crevasses.

We reached the top of the glacier. Our boots crunched in the corn snow, warmed by the sun. I had been watching our back-track to make sure we were making footprints that we could follow down. We found ourselves facing a strong wind coming from the north. In the vast expanse of white snow, I spotted a singular rock outcropping about a hundred yards ahead.

"Let's hunker down behind that rock out of the wind," I said, "and have a snack."

Walt nodded. I noted he remained in good shape after our long climb.

We pulled off our packs and sat on the snow, out of the wind, and rested. Walt pulled a tangerine from his pack and offered it to me. "Oh boy, just what I need. Here, I'll split it with you."

"No, it's okay. I got another one. I was expecting company." He smiled showing a sense of humor that was welcome in this arena of constant physical torment.

We sat shoulder to shoulder, hoods up against the wind that was whistling around the rock against which we rested. We peeled the tangerines and ate them, savoring the meat and juices of each segment until they were all gone.

We rested panting against the rock. Looking down over the expanse to the glacier we'd just climbed, I pointed out that none of the crevasses could be seen from this angle. From this height we could see forever in the thin air.

"Zowee, that was good," Walt said. "Never tasted better. I got another. Want to split it?"

"I'd love to, but we better wait until we reach the summit. We might need it. We still got a long way to go."

We looked across a wide saddle to the main crater about a mile away. "Over there to our left at about a quarter mile range is a hump that I recognize from photos as a blown-out remnant of a crater. To our front is another hump that must be the second crater that got blown away when Rainier blew its top eons ago and formed most of the lower Cascade Mountains. To our right front at a range of two miles or so, up that rise you can see a mesa-like looking mass that must be the rim of the remaining crater. Somewhere along the rim of the crater is the highest point of the mountain at 14,406 feet." (More recently surveyed at 14,410 feet.)

Dressed in nylon parkas, wearing crampons on our feet and glacier goggles to protect our eyes, we began the long walk up the final slope of the peak of Mount Rainier. A stiff wind blew at our backs helping us on as we struggled to keep the climbing rope taut between us.

Finally we reached the crest of the one surviving crater. From here we could get better perspective on distances because I knew the crater was about a quarter mile across.

"Look back. We've come more than a mile across the top of this mountain."

Walt nodded in agreement.

"There is a metal cylinder containing a log where we are supposed to register at the very summit of the mountain. Can you tell from our position on the rim, where it might be?"

Walt studied the crater. Finally he pointed to a place on the eastern side. I agreed and took a compass reading. We started to walk along the rim. I didn't notice the wind shifting from north to south-west.

Soon after we started walking the mountain socked in. When I realized what was happening I took another compass reading. Within minutes we could barely see each other at conversation distance.

"What do we do now?" Walt said.

"I got a pretty good fix on where we are in terms of where we first came up on the rim. We should continue to follow it.

When the wind is at our backs we should be close to the capsule that contains the register."

"Okay."

With the fog and the wind and the wind shift, the temperature dropped dramatically. Soon it was cold enough that my canteen froze solid. Hoar frost formed on our faces.

"This is what happens when a mushroom-shaped cloud cap forms over the peak. We need to go down and soon. We'll freeze to death if we stay here."

We worked our way around the crater until the wind was dead at our backs again. We hadn't found the canister.

"Walt, to the best I can figure, this is where we came up to the crater. I'm going to head directly down wind and hope we're close to the right course. You wait here until you feel the rope draw taut. Then proceed keeping the rope taut. Let me pull you along. We started down. I checked my compass frequently. We were following a north by west course. When the slope steepened, I corrected to maintain a steady downward course. I didn't want to enter the top of the Kautz Glacier too soon for fear of stepping into a crevasse. We walked on like this for nearly an hour, our only contact the pull of the climbing rope.

The wind died with a suddenness that made me stumble. In the silence I realized how noisily the wind had been shrieking. It seemed warmer. I moved onward, squinting my eyes against the ice crystals forming on my lids. I peered forward, straining to see in the dense fog. I had no idea where on the mountain we were.

I spotted something darker than the surrounding gray. We approached a rock outcropping and I saw, scattered on the ice, tangerine peelings obviously left by Walt and me on our way up.

"Walt, Walt, come up quickly. I've found where we rested and ate the tangerines. I don't believe it. It's almost miraculous. Do you know what this means?"

"Yeah. We should be able to follow our tracks back down through the glacier. Wanna share a tangerine to celebrate?"

"You bet. Dig it out while I look for tracks." We remained roped up while I circled. Soon I gave a "whoopee. Found 'em." I walked back to the rock which I could see plainly now. The fog was lifting.

We sat on the rocky outcrop and ate half-frozen tangerine wedges. Nothing ever tasted better. While we sat, the fog lifted enough so that we sat under a ceiling of heavy clouds looking down over the glacier.

"We'll take turns leading. I'll start. I'll follow our tracks as closely as I can. Step only where I have trod. You understand?"

"You betchum, Red Ryder.'

The going downward was deceptively easier at the start. As our thighs began to burn and fatigue set in, we grew cautious not to overstep ourselves and take a tumble. When we reached the ice fall we used extreme caution, belaying each other all the way down.

We arrived at the basecamp. While the stay-behinds packed up, I briefed Bill on our successful climb.

"You are a couple of lucky guys. You should have holed up in the ice caves that lie just below the inside of the crater."

"I thought about that, Bill, but I never saw any and the cold was getting so bad we had to keep moving."

"Well, you sure got a guardian angel watching out for you. Let's go down."

The rest of the climb was an easy glissade down the Nisqually glacier.

Greywolf Encounter

When I was younger, I decided to explore the Olympic Mountains on my own. I planned to drive to the end of the road at Dungeness Forks camp. The map showed the Greywolf River flowed down into the Dungeness River through high mountain passes near Highway 101, overlooking the straits of Juan de Fuca. There should be some fine summer steelhead fishing up the river.

I crossed the Dungeness on a fallen fir tree bole, offering a bridge and access to the mouth of the Greywolf. There was a game trail. I followed the river upward to the beginning of the Olympic National Park and a long twisting climb into a narrow pass far above the river. At timberline I stood on an outcropping and looked up into the Olympic peaks and then straight down to the river far below me. A Bald Eagle soared below me. What a glorious sight.

The trail gradually descended from there until it eventually joined the river in a rain forest. It was very quiet. No sounds of birds or insects. Only the steady drip of raindrops falling from cedars onto a surface of Devil's Club, Vine Maple, and moss covered rotting cedar trunks lying about like so many corpses, their bare branches like arms lying akimbo. Spooky. The rain fell straight down, soaking everything.

The trail joined the river along a calm run.

I investigated what appeared to be an old campsite, long deserted. A weathered wooden sign was tacked to a tree. It looked like the remains of a bulletin board. Its top displayed the faded letters "CCC." I remembered my Dad telling me about his days in Franklin Roosevelt's Civilian Conservation Corps. There were several sets of initials carved into the face of the board, dating back to the early 1930s.

I circled until I found a live cedar tree, its branches protecting a relatively dry area around its base.

This will be my camp. Let's see if I can catch my supper.

I unpacked my old three piece bamboo fly rod and walked to the edge of the river. I found myself beside a small waterfall, below which there was a deep eddying pool. Baiting my hook with a single salmon egg, I cast into the water. A strike bent my rod nearly double. The surface of the water exploded as a big steelhead emerged from the depths. I fought it with gusto as it fought my hook. When it finally tired, I lifted its head up and scooped it onto the rocks. Beautiful. I carefully unhooked it and led it through ankle-deep water until it revived and hurried away.

"Goodbye, Mister Steelhead," I said aloud. "Thank you."

More casting brought in a few brook trout for supper.

I needed to start a fire. It would be difficult in the rain forest. I looked about and found a fallen cedar tree trunk hollowed out by ants. Inside were layers of paper thin wood, fairly dry. Gathering dead twigs from the bottoms of fir trees, I managed to start a flame and soon was roasting my fish and warming a can of beans.

I leaned against my cedar tree in the approaching twilight watching the now red hot coals and sipping a steaming cup of tea. Darkness fell. The rain stopped. Looking up through the branches of the cedar I saw stars. I felt at peace with the world.

Gradually I came to realize I was not alone. In the flickering light cast by my fire sat a big cougar. It sat at the very edge of the firelight watching me intently. It made no movement.

I was startled, seeing the cat so close. At first I was mightily spooked. Then I felt a certain comfort in knowing I was no longer alone in the world. Somehow I knew the cougar presented no threat to me. It was merely curious.

"Well, Mister Cougar," I said aloud, "It's nice to make your acquaintance. If you don't mind, my supper is ready. I'll have to think about whether I offer to share it with you."

I moved about the fire, keeping an eye on the cougar.

The big cat remained motionless.

I wasn't frightened. His eyes, reflecting the firelight, held me enthralled.

When I turned in for the night the Cougar had disappeared.

"Good night, Mister Cat. I enjoyed your visit."

I slept soundly that night and when I woke in the morning I discovered cougar tracks circling my tree.

I hiked on up into the Olympic range for three more days. I saw elk and mountain goats, but the cougar had disappeared from my life forever. That cat made my trip a success by sharing a bit of its day with me.

SEARCH FOR GOLD

Each morning I search for Gold
In my garden
I pour a cup of coffee
And walk out to my pond
I walk softly
Stepping oh so slowly
Hoping to see Gold
And lo! There she is
Floating deep in my pond
Her frond-like fins
Waving ever so slowly
She moves like a nymph
Through the crystalline waters
Like a Goddess
And I am enchanted

The Ballad of Suzie and Sammie

"Dick! Come out here quick!" Brenda called to me from the patio. I was just finishing my second cup of coffee. The outside door from the kitchen was open. It was a lovely June morning; rare in the Pacific Northwest.

"What's the matter?" I asked starting up, and heading for the door.

"I think there's a duck on the roof," she said. I slowed a bit with the knowledge that all of Lakewood wasn't burning down. I smiled as I thought of the beginnings of a poem: *Dick, come quick! I think there's a duck on . . .,* well maybe just a limerick.

I stepped out onto the patio, looked up where Brenda was pointing, and sure enough, there on the shakes stood a female Mallard.

Nervously she looked us over. "Quack," she said.

"Let's go inside. Maybe she'll come down," Brenda said.

"By all means," I said as we moved toward the door.

Brenda loved all birds. Our house, wherever it might be, was always a bird sanctuary. Lord help the cat who came bird-hunting around our place.

After a bit, sure enough, the duck flew down to the patio floor. She looked about, gave a couple of satisfied chortles which sounded amazingly like, "quack, quack."

Then she waddled straight for the door.

"I'll get a slice of bread. Maybe she'll eat it," said Brenda excitedly. "Maybe I should get some water, too." Not many things excited Brenda. One thing that did was the presence of birds.

After eating some of the bread, Suzie, as my wife immediately named her, took a few sips of water. Then she flew away toward a nearby pond.

The next day she was back. We observed pretty much the same scenario.

On the third day she came again. This time she had a beautiful Mallard drake in tow. Brenda immediately dubbed him "Sammy."

We, my wife Brenda and I, spent summer afternoons lounging in our very private back yard at a house we owned in the Lakewood suburb of Tacoma, Washington. I had bricked in the patio and planted rhododendrons to augment the mountain laurels and the several mature Doulas Firs that surrounded the house. The evergreen shrubbery was reinforced by platoons of flowers. It was a very private place. It was our quiet place, until that day when we began sharing it with Suzie and Sammy.

Suzie, She Who Was to be Obeyed, took immediate possession of the lawn, waddling about on what was to become her daily inspection tour, bobbing her head to and fro, and occasionally giving orders to Sammy.

"M-mrack, ckk, ckk," she'd say.

Sammy, resplendent in his iridescent green, blue, and white mating plumage, responded with a dip of his beak and, "R-r-r-uck, ruck," as he followed her about, being careful to remain positioned between his lovely mate and us, protecting her from possible harm.

Brenda and I wondered why they picked this place to land. We discussed it *ad nauseum*, during the remainder of the summer we shared our home with the pair of Mallards. They returned again on the second day, and when they returned on the third day, we noticed Sammy was a good flyer, totally in control during landings. He usually flared into a stall just as his feet touched down on the grass. Most often he made it a three point landing by skidding to a stop on his derriere.

Suzie, on the other hand, tended to come in too hot, skidding on her belly, and twice out of three attempts, spinning head over tea kettle.

On the third day, we noticed that Suzie had picked up a splinter, a big one, in her left foot. To say that it was a splinter is an understatement. It was more like a straw-colored twig that extended from somewhere in the center of her foot to beyond the webbing between her toes. She presented herself as the legendary lame duck incarnate.

Thenceforth, for the remainder of the summer, each evening, shortly after sundown, Suzie would commence her departure ritual. She waddled toward the front yard, and then skittered sideways in both directions a few feet. Sammy followed a pace or two to the rear. Both ducks sounded off with an authoritative, "qua-a-ack, quack."

When Suzie had her take-off line properly set up between the trees, she'd waggle her head at Sammy and off they'd go, heading, we presumed for one of the two small lakes that lay close by our home.

We wondered if they were raising a family at lakeside, and retreated to our house for a mid-afternoon break from parenting.

At night our pillow-talk focused on the Mallard pair. Brenda said, "Suzie has got to be in a lot of pain because of that foot."

"Yes. I wonder if that's why she makes such bad landings, or if her lack of landing skill was the cause of her problem. At any rate she probably tried to land among some rushes and picked up the splinter in the process."

"Can't we do something for her?"

"If they come back tomorrow I'll try to catch her and pull the splinter out."

"Maybe," Brenda said, "we should try to make some kind of pond for them."

Wide awake now, I could see this was quickly becoming a second career for me. I imagined the "Angel of Worries" looking down on us and thinking, *Aha, there's Dick, recently retired from Army service, and just finished remodeling his house. Kids all grown up and flown the nest. He thinks he hasn't got a worry in the world. I'll just show him it doesn't work that way for the living. The Mallard family needs a little help.*

The next morning I hunted around in the garage, searching out and finding my salmon net and an old, unused dishpan. I pounded out the bigger dents. Then I dug a hole in the back yard and sank the pan in it to provide a reasonable facsimile of the ol' swimmin' hole for Mister and Missus Mallard. Satisfied it would serve, I filled it with fresh water.

That afternoon Brenda and I waited impatiently for the ducks to arrive. I watered the lawn attempting to literally grease the skids for landing. Brenda stood by with antiseptic and bandages. I fingered my salmon net with which I planned to ensnare Suzie.

They showed at the scheduled time, Suzie in the lead as usual. She made her approach at warp speed, and settled onto the lawn like an F-4 making a cross-wind landing on an aircraft carrier. She skidded to a stop on her belly.

After Sammy glided to a perfect three point landing, she began limping about, looking for something to eat in the grass. We noticed that her gait had worsened.

We swung into action. Brenda circled to the left, arms spread wide. I circled to the right. Suzie retreated under a bush. Sammy observed the action calmly from under a lawn chair. Suzie started quacking.

On the third try I managed to get the net over Suzie. I planted its metal hoop firmly on the ground and scooped her up. Feathers flew. Brenda managed to get both her hands on Suzie's body. She hugged the duck close, trying not to hurt her.

I threw the net aside, and as Brenda held her, took her left foot firmly in my left hand and with my right fingers, deftly extracted the splinter. I say deftly. Actually it came out with ease.

Suzie immediately stopped squirming and quacking. She lay quietly in Brenda's hands. Brenda handed her to me and began to wash the duck's appendage with antiseptic. She inspected the foot for any remaining splinters, and wrapped it with water-proof tape.

Placed back on the turf, Suzie calmly walked to the dishpan-cum-swimming pool, flopped into it, and began swimming around contentedly. Sammy waddled over to join her. I imagined the Angel of Worries as he or she or whatever, placed gold stars on our service records.

The Mallards made our back yard their summer palace for the rest of that warm season. We accepted them as part of our family, and looked forward each day to their arrival.

The normal drill was for Brenda and me to sit relaxing on the patio enjoying a cooling drink until Suzie and Sammy arrived. They'd land (Suzie's landing skill had improved somewhat) and walk about for a while. Then she'd pop into the pool for a quick dunk before the two of them settled under a bush, and roosted until late afternoon when it was time for their departure.

When the weather turned hot they spent hours nesting under the laurels in our back yard. As the weeks went by, they ranged outward from our yard into the streets, waddling awkwardly, in search of whatever it was she was looking for. It must have been food, but I couldn't, for the life of me, figure out what it was she was finding to eat in the gutters along the road.

We lived on a corner lot. A through-street ran along one side of our house and crossed a cul-de-sac that ran in front of the house. As Suzie ranged up and down the streets, scouring the bottoms of the roadside ditches,

Sammy rode shotgun along the edges of the tarmac, keeping careful watch over his comely bride.

We worried about their safety, especially on the busier through-street. I tried to keep them on the cul-de-sac where there was hardly any traffic. When I spotted Sammy on the wrong road I'd herd them both back onto the cul-de-sac in the front of the house.

One day, I was working in the front yard while Suzie was working the gutters, when a car passed at a fairly high rate of speed. I heard one of the ducks give a loud squawk. Looking up I saw a cloud of feathers flying near the edge of the road. Hurrying over I found Sammy's broken body in the ditch.

The car was nowhere to be seen. Neither was Suzie.

Gathering up poor Sammy, I saw he was still alive, but with one wing hanging limply, and one of his thighs shattered. There was no telling what injuries he sustained internally. Tears clouded my eyes as I carried him carefully into the back yard and placed him under a laurel bush to die.

I knew he had to be in great pain. I hoped he would die quickly.

Brenda and I waited for Suzie to come back, but she never returned that day.

The next morning when I got out of bed, I dressed and went out to see to Sammy. He hadn't moved from the position in which I placed him. Unfortunately he was still alive. There was nothing to do, but put him quickly out of his misery. I tearfully, prayerfully dispatched him, and buried him in the yard.

We mourned him the rest of the summer.

At the beginning of fall, Suzie returned with a new partner. Her foot was totally healed, but her landings hadn't improved very much. We welcomed her and tolerated her new beau, but we couldn't bear to name him. Things just could never be quite the same.

After a few days, the ducks disappeared, probably to fly south for the winter. We never saw Suzie again.

Now, whenever we see Mallards we think of the ducks that enriched our lives for a summer by sharing theirs with us. All these years, Suzie and Sammy have remained in our hearts as part of our family. Whenever Brenda sees Mallards flying overhead she points to them and says ritually, "There go Suzie and Sammy."

The Bummer

In 1970, while I was stationed at Fort Lewis, Washington, I did a lot of steelhead fishing in the Nisqually River, which forms the southern boundary of the military reservation. On the other side of the river lies the Nisqually Indian Reservation. One day after fishing I found a young pup wandering in the woods. He looked lost and hungry, so I took him home. I found out later he was half Malamute and half wolf. My family of five adopted him—or he adopted us, and stayed with us through fourteen years of assignments to Alaska, Minnesota, and Kansas. He lived for fourteen years and then died. Here is his story from his own perspective.

It is morning. I hear my human father coming; the alpha-male of my pack. His feet make crunching sounds in the snow outside.

I am filled with joy, anticipating the feel of his warm hands in my coat.

Here he is!

He kneels on the frozen cement, takes me in his arms and speaks to me in loving tones.

"Good morning, my sweet boy. I love you, Bummer. I wish we didn't have to keep you out here in the cold all night."

I wish not to look weak, but I can't help myself. I'm shaking all over and mewling like a puppy. I lick his face. His skin tastes warm. I feel and understand rather than hear what he is saying to me.

I wish I could make him understand I know why I have to spend the nights outside in the shed where the automobiles are kept. I don't want to relieve myself inside our living place. I try and try to hold it until the morning, but I am unable to keep my soilage within myself.

"C'mon boy. Let's get warmed up and have some breakfast."

We start for the house. I feel wonderful. Here I am beside my human. He twirls his fingers in the curl of my tail as he has done most of my life. We move toward the door of our living place.

"Honey! Here we are. Here's our Bummer, hungry as hell."

He kneels before me and begins to rub the cold from my fur. I sit and smell the grand smells of the family. I hear the sounds of everyone waking up. I hope the alpha does not discover I cannot see them anymore.

Seeing is very important to my humans, but smelling and hearing is more important to me. I can do very well without seeing. I don't want the alpha to sense that. I don't know why.

The female, she who is most like my birth mother, comes out of the kitchen and kneels to stroke my fur. This is the touch of one who counts above all others to me. My life has been dedicated to protecting her and those she loves from harm.

She places my feeding bowl on the floor. I gobble it down gratefully if not gracefully.

"Oh, Bummer. My beautiful Bummer. How I wish you could be a puppy again."

She is crying. I feel a sadness about her that is reflected in the Alpha. She releases me and stands to be held closely by alpha. I growl softly, hoping he doesn't hear my feelings being expressed. I mean him no harm. I worship him.

"Oh Dick," she says, "I wish this day would never have come."

"I know, Sweetheart. I'd give anything not to have to take him in to the vet today. But it's time."

They are speaking very seriously. I feel rather than understand that something terrible is about to occur.

"But, Dick. Isn't there something else we can do? Something we haven't thought of?"

"Honey, he's fourteen. He's lived a good life. He can't control his bodily functions any more. He's nearly blind. If there was another way, you know I would jump on it. He's gotta be in a lot of pain. It's time."

Sensing that they are communicating some very serious thing about me, I take immediate action. Though it causes me incredible pain, I jump up and run to the door. I bark loudly to be let outside.

"Well, I'll be damned," the Alpha says, "I haven't heard him bark like that since we moved from Alaska."

"What's he barking at?"

"Dunno," says the Alpha.,

He looks out the window.

"Hey, there's a squirrel."

The door is opened and I immediately begin stalking the squirrel. I can smell it nearby. It hears or sees me approaching and begins its alarm call.

Cool, as is my style, I creep up into striking range and lunge at the squirrel. He jumps up the trunk of a tree. I catch him. Dropping back to the ground, I proudly sport my kill. It has been thus all my life and is so even now.

"Holy smoke, Baby. Did'ja see that? He's acting like he did five years ago. I've never seen him move faster."

"Yes, dear, I saw that. Maybe we're being too hasty in our decision to put him down."

"Maybe you're right. Let's put it off for a few days. I'll call the vet."

I hastily consume my kill, which is the way of my pack, and prance up and down the yard, proudly proclaiming my accomplishment. Both my humans rush out to stroke me and praise me.

I feel young again.

Tonight, I lay on my pallet in the hut among the automobiles. I'm thinking back to when I began to be. I can remember very clearly the day I was born. I remember the sounds and smells of my mother. She was the canine mistress of the world. I don't remember anything of my father, but I was assured that he was big and strong.

I huddled in the dark with my brothers and sisters. When my mother cuddled around us, we all started to cry and prance about. We ran to her and jumped, reaching for her nipples. I hung back and welcomed her with a lick on her nose. She lay on her side and offered her breasts to us. All rushed to feed. But I was content to nuzzle my mother's nose. When I had properly greeted her, I sauntered over and pushed my way through the pack, feeding at leisure.

When we could see, our human let us go outdoors to play. The smells and sounds of the world assaulted our senses. Mother watched over us as we explored our universe.

The river especially drew me. Its movement and incessant roiling provided a constant thrill as it rushed to the salt water in front our home place.

Mother said I must never go near the river. Danger lurked on the other side. It's true. Often I heard deep rumbling noises coming from there.

She taught us about the dangers of the moving sheds that rolled about our land. They stank and made a great noise. Automobiles, she called them.

Whenever we broke some pack rule she snapped at us and bit down on our necks, just hard enough to get our attention.

One day our human alpha-male had a visitor. He came storming up in his automobile, just missing one of my brothers. I don't know what they were talking about, but I know it concerned us.

"These sure are a lively pack of pups, Nathan. Look at how their tails curl like so many bushes blowing in the wind. What breed d'ja say they are?"

"The mother is pure-bred malamute. The sire is a wolf hybrid. Big sucker."

"Yeah, by the looks of their paws, I'd say the pups are sure gonna be big. They'll make great work dogs. Any of them spoken for yet?"

"Naw. You're the first to see them."

"You gonna keep any?"

"Not sure. By Nisqually tribal rules I hafta offer them free to any member of the tribe before I sell them off the reservation. They're so good lookin' I might keep at least one female. And that big male there, ya see him? He moves like he owns the place. He'll be the alpha-male of this litter for sure. I like him."

I knew they were pointing at me and I tried to stand tall, marching about until I tripped over a root. I pretended to stalk a squirrel to make it look like my fall was planned. One of my brothers joined in on the hunt until I sent him packing with a growl and a snap of my baby teeth.

"Bet you could get a good price for them in Steilacoom or at the Army post across the river."

"Don't get me started on the Army, John. Day and night now they're firin' those damn howitzers. The impact area seems to be moving closer to the river. Getting so a man can't sleep."

The days grew longer as the sun climbed higher each day. More strangers came in their stinky automobiles. Some of them picked me up with unfriendly hands to poke at my ribs and belly. When I resisted by growling and showing my emerging fangs, my alpha-human cuffed me and spoke angry words I didn't understand.

Mostly, though, we pups were left to our own games and exploring our universe. I liked to chase field mice, voles, and ground squirrels. Each of them taunted me in its own way until one day, quite by accident, I caught a squirrel. I was as surprised as it was. I dropped it. The squirrel huddled on the ground screaming.

Still surprised, I sniff at it. It nips me on the nose. Angered now, I grab the squirrel in my teeth and bite down.

193

I feel its little bones crack. Then the taste of its blood tells me I have found a new source of food.

I pranced about, showing off my kill to my brothers and sisters. Then I set about eating it, bones and all. My brothers and sisters, each in their turn, came sniffing around to see if there was something here for them to eat. My growls drove them away.

Dark periods followed by light went by, and the summer sun shined down warmly. My confidence expanded. I studied the river. At night I heard the rumblings of what I was told were horrible beasts on the other side. I was afraid, yet not afraid. I wanted to see these beasts. They will be no match for me. I grew bigger every day.

I climbed a rock overhanging the river. I sat on the summit looking down at the water rushing by. I felt like a king. King of the rock. King of all I survey. A flash of silver from within the river caught my eye. Looking down intently, I watched as a creature broke the surface of the river and splashed water on me.

I couldn't resist. I lunged toward the creature. I was surprised to find the surface didn't support my weight. I was engulfed by the river. I tried to bark, but my mouth was full of water. I struck out in all directions with my paws. As quickly as I sank, I bobbed to the surface, choking for air.

I drifted along as fast as the surface of the river, watching the shore speed by. I moved and kicked my legs. Air filled my lungs as I struck out for the shore.

I was knocked dizzy as my head hit a rock. I clung to it and crawled up and out of the river. The river strove to hold me in its clutches and called for me to rejoin it.

Looking around, fur dripping, panting, I discovered that I was on the other side of the river.

I caught my breath while I studied the woods. This looked very much like my side of the river, except there were no sheds or creatures moving about; only the deep darkness of some strange place.

I moved away from the shore and shook myself vigorously to rid my fur of water.

Darkness fell.

I looked for cover. The rumblings of the unknown beasts were beginning and I was a little afraid. I curled up under a bush to sleep.

I was awakened by a squirrel, standing just before me. It darted back and forth and scolded me for being there. I pretended to sleep. The squirrel grew bold and approached. Momentarily I struck, pinning it with my forepaws and biting down until I heard its bones crack.

Chewing on my breakfast, I looked about. I had yet to see any of the beasts that created the rumblings. I decided to go and search for them.

I penetrated deeper into the woods. I wasn't sure I could find my way back to the river. After a while the woods thinned out and the land appeared sere and blackened. I continued on.

Everything smelled stinky like the automobiles. It was so strong my nostrils were filled with it.

I heard a loud *whooosh!* The sound grew louder. I cowered beneath the blackened branches of what must once have been a bush.

The sound increased and built to a scream, stopped suddenly, and after no more that a short second, there was an ear-splitting "Ka-voom!" Rocks and trees were thrown about. No sooner did I realize I have survived this, when another upheaval occurred.

Then another.

I cowered in the dust, shivering with fear.

I ran like I have never run before. I ran until I could run no more. I reached the green forest; I dropped beneath the protective cover of a tree to sleep.

Sometime later I awoke to the sound of a human walking. I crouched down, but the footsteps did not approach. They stopped.

I moved forward, eyes straining to see who was there. Peeking out from behind a bush, I saw a human standing beside one of the automobiles I have seen near my home.

I studied him closely. He appeared different from my own humans. His hide was lighter. His hair was shorter.

He noticed me.

He looked closely at me.

"Hey, fella. Are you a dog or a coyote?"

I shrank back among the branches.

He continued to talk to me softly—strangely.

"Aw. C'mon boy. Let's get a look at you. I'll bet you're hungry aren't you."

I was drawn to him in a way I cannot explain. I moved tentatively toward him. All my confidence was gone. I moved closer and let him touch me. His hands were warm and confident. They told me he was my friend.

"You're kinda skinny aren't you? Definitely a dog. Some sort of Husky."

His words were soothing as he stroked my back.

"Where do you come from? Bet you swam across from the Indian side of the river."

He twirled my tail with his fingers in a playful way that made me jump back.

"It's okay, fella. I won't hurt you."

I returned to his open arms and he lifted me up and placed me in his automobile.

Frightened, I growled and snapped at him. I didn't want to hurt him, but I couldn't help myself.

"Whoa! You act like you've never been in a truck before."

His hand was bleeding. He had me trapped in the "truck." I cowered in a corner waiting for him to strike me.

He reached for something, maybe a weapon, picked up a cloth and wrapped his bleeding hand.

"What a bummer. Yep, that's what I'll call you. Bummer. Don't be afraid, boy. I'm not gonna hurt you."

He sat beside me in the truck and pushed little black buttons until the truck vibrated, rumbled, and began to move across the ground.

Terrified, I hide my head in a corner.

We moved slowly at first; then faster as the ground suddenly became smoother. I heard strange noises outside. It smelled different. I was still frightened, but now I was curious.

This human's seat stretched across the truck to beside me. Propping my front paws on the seat, I lifted my head up so I could see out.

I was amazed.

I saw all sorts of trucks and automobiles, all speeding by. I jumped up on the seat and gazed about me. I was enthralled. There were gigantic sheds all around—and countless people.

"That's a good boy. New to this kind of territory aren't you, Bummer, boy? We'll be home soon."

I looked at everything speeding by. Pretty soon we slowed down and pulled up beside a shed. Two small humans came running up to the truck as it stopped. The rumbling quieted and my human left the truck, closing the door behind him.

"Daddy, Daddy! Did you catch any fish?"

"Not this time, but I did catch something more interesting. Look in the truck."

A female human peered through the glass. When she saw me, she squealed.

"Oh, Daddy! It's a dog! Whee-e-e-e! Can we keep it? What's its name?"

Both the small humans were jumping up and down. I was frightened.

"We'll have to ask your mommy. But this dog probably belongs to somebody. They'll want him back. We'll have to see."

My human opened the door and reached for me. I started to bite him, but then decided not to. I was beginning to trust him. He picked me up in his arms. They felt warm and comforting.

"Now, boy. You gotta be on your good behavior."

We entered the nearby shed.

"Hi, Honey. I'm home. Look what I found at the river."

A female human entered our space. She smelled good and there were better scents coming with her from another section of the shed. I started to salivate.

"Oh my goodness. What have we here? Dick this looks like a valuable dog. We aren't going to keep him are we? You've been hurt. Did this dog do that?"

The small humans were jumping around again. I jumped with them.

"Oh please, Mommy. Please. Can't we keep him?"

"Quiet down, kids. We're going to take him to the vet for a checkup. After that we have to try to try to find his owner. Somebody must be missing him."

No one ever claimed me and I became one of the family. I learned that the deep rumbling was the noise from big guns being fired by the soldiers who inhabit this place. My alpha human is a soldier.

A short time after I came to live with my human family, I heard the alpha talking with the mother about me.

"I'm going steelheading in the morning. I think I'll take the Bummer along with me."

"Oh, no. What if he goes back to the reservation?"

"If he crosses back over the river, so be it. Better to know now if he will stay with us. If he wanders, we want to know before we commit to him totally."

"It's already too late for the children. They love him. I do too."

The next morning, my alpha loaded up the truck with fishing gear. I watched as he added a metal bottle filled with hot liquid.

"Okay, boy. Hop up and let's go."

Joyfully, I sprang up on the seat. I'd ridden enough in the truck to be accustomed to it. I was no longer afraid. We were about to embark on an exciting adventure. I knew it.

Alpha drove the truck through the Army post and out into the woods. Soon we came upon terrain that seemed familiar to me. I heard the rushing sound of the river.

We stopped and I looked at the woods through the window. Alpha opened the door and got out.

"Well, come on. The fish are waiting."

I hopped down and Alpha retrieved his gear from the bed of the truck. He spent several minutes fussing with stuff in the back of the truck and then we headed for the river. I hung back, not knowing what was expected of me.

"Come on, Bummer. Let's look for a good place to fish."

We walked along the river bank. I was excited by the noise of the water rushing by. We stopped at a likely looking pool where I sensed the water must be deep.

Alpha affixed some salmon roe onto a stick. The smell of it excited me. He swung his whip-like stick back and cast his roe far out into the river.

I climbed up to the top of a near-by rock and watched expectantly. Nothing happened. Several times more he cast into the pool.

"We better add some weight. We're not getting down deep enough. Bummer? Bummer where are you? Oh there you are. How'd you get up on that rock? Can you see better up there?"

I looked down on Alpha. He looked up at me and smiled. Then he cast into the river again. I watched expectantly. Nothing. I sat down to watch and wait. My Human was enjoying himself. I rejoiced with him, in the day.

I saw a flash of silver, deep within the rushing waters. I stood as Alpha tensed and his stick bent nearly double.

"Yahoo! Fish on!"

A great fish broke the surface in the middle of the pool. I watched closely as it struggled against the line. Alpha moved up and down the bank with the movements of the steelhead.

"Oh, Bummer! This is a beauty. Must go fifteen pounds. Yahoo!"

The fish ran quickly up and down the river several times. Then it stopped to rest just below me. I couldn't resist. I leaped, sailing out and over the pool, like the large birds I have seen, I was flying and then diving into the water to catch a fish.

I landed on the water with a great splash. I struck out with my fangs at the fish, but it was gone.

The water gripped me closely and I was reminded of a time before when I bobbed about in the river at its mercy.

I moved quickly down the river. I saw the Alpha running along the bank, trying to keep up with me. He was shouting, why I did not know.

The river carried me to a quiet place filled with logs, bobbing up and down. I tried to climb over them to the shore, but I couldn't manage it.

The Alpha appeared and reached for me. He grasped a hand full of my fur and pulled me to him. He lost his footing and was about to topple into the river with me.

Momentarily I thought *oh what fun we will have.* Then I sensed his panic. My joy turned to fear. I scrambled into his arms. His clothes turned wet with the touch of my fur.

"Bummer, you bummer! Oh come here my boy! We'll get you out of there!"

He hugged me close. His warmth was reflected by my thick fur. Together we rejoiced at the quickness of life. We were both soaked. He knelt and set me down. I gave a great shake. Then I shook again.

"Oh great! Now I'm even wetter! Listen you Bummer! If you do that again I'll leave you to get out of the river on your own!"

He shook his finger at me and I was afraid.

Again he hugged me close and I knew he loved me. I loved him.

I sensed this was the beginning of a great adventure of life. I licked his face.

As I grew bigger and stronger, we moved to a far land I heard my humans call "Alaska." While there I had many adventures, always in the company of my family.

Much time has passed and the small humans have grown up. I love my human family and I know they love me. But I feel the time is coming very soon that I must go wherever we go when the breath of life leaves forever. It has been good.

Sasquatch

I worked for hours pulling scotch broom one cloudy day in May. I had declared war on the noxious weed some ten years before. I was determined to eliminate it from my property. Every spring it returned, admittedly in diminishing numbers, and bloomed in bright yellow blossoms, thus highlighting its presence. I, with my trusty weed puller would commence another campaign, pulling and burning.

Occasionally I mounted a foray against the blackberry bushes, but mostly we maintained an easy truce. The vines kept their distance and they produced succulent fruit each year for my grandchildren to pick, for my wife to make prize-winning cobbler, and for me to eat with lots of whipped cream.

This year it appeared I was about to win the war. All that remained after four days of battle were a few scattered bushes in the undeveloped acre behind my house.

My property adjoined the back of Joemma State Park on the edge of some wild acreage that, together with my back-land consisted largely of vine maple, devil's club, and blackberries, making it very difficult to negotiate. Whenever I went back there I carried a machete and wielded it indiscriminately.

There were also plants like columbine, Oregon grape, and trillium to be discovered like jewels among the weeds.

Occasionally I'd find a fully grown scotch broom, previously undiscovered in my travels about the property.

Once I found a depression back there that looked to be human size. I was tempted to dig in it, but opined it might be an Indian grave. If so, better to leave it be.

My wife Brenda kept close watch on my efforts.

"Dick, you be careful out there. Don't overdo. You've got your inhaler?"

She suffered from COPD and feared my getting winded might cause me to have an asthma attack.

"Yes, Honey, don't fret. Got it right here in my pocket."

She worried more if I wandered out of her sight. If she knew I was going into the back woods she'd caution me to be careful and not be gone long.

"Sweetheart," I said to her as I entered the kitchen for a glass of water, "I think I've got that nasty scotch broom about licked for this year. Looks like we're gonna have a good crop of blackberries. Yum. I can smell the cobbler already.

"I just need to take a look out back. Don't worry, I've got my inhaler with me and I'll take my trusty machete."

"Please be careful. We've been hearing coyotes close by the last few nights. They worry me. Are you taking Sandy with you?"

"No. She'll just get under foot. Besides, she's worked hard all morning guarding me from errant squirrels and ferocious chipmunks. Let her take a nap with you. I won't be long."

I kissed her and hugged her as close as I dared.

"Just be careful," she said breathlessly, brushing my hair back.

I stepped off the deck and into the woods, clearing last year's path, swinging my machete as I went. The blackberries had thrown suckers across the trail.

"Hey, guys. You're in violation of our mutual nonintervention pact." I swung the machete on both sides of the trail to sever the errant vines.

I looked from side to side, searching for the tell-tale yellow blossoms. I glanced to the ground often, careful not to step on trillium and other forest delicacies.

I stopped short of a rotting log and looked for spore in a patch of muddy soil on the farther side of the deadfall. There was the fresh track of a large deer. I studied the footprint, looking for signs of other animals that might be frequenting my backyard. Finding none, I stood and was about to step over the log when I spotted it; an impression of a large bare human foot, at least twice the size of my own foot.

Awestruck, I studied the print for some moments. *Was this a bear?* There were several in the neighborhood. *No. Too big and not the right shape. What could it be?* I dared not think it might be the mark of the fabled Sasquatch.

The legend of Bigfoot had been growing stronger of recent years, but for all my wandering alone in the Cascades and Olympics, I had never once seen any sign of the fabled creature.

I decided to follow this trail and moved in the direction it led. A few paces forward I found, thanks to my Boy Scout training, a few bent twigs indicating the passage of a large animal. They told me I was on the trail of whatever this creature was.

I moved forward into ever-thicker brush, keeping my eye to the ground. The brambles seemed to reach out and grasp my ankles, my arms. The going got tougher. I was sweating profusely. Every so often I thought I saw movement from the corner of my eye. I glanced up, but saw only silent forest. I found no further tracks.

Struggling on though the morass, I spotted the stump of one of the aboriginal firs. It was huge—some eight or ten feet across and completely covered with salal and huckleberry. Near the ground there appeared to be the opening of a burrow, large enough for a bear.

I worked my way closer, trying to see into the burrow.

I was breathing hard and sweating. Yellow jackets, buzzed around my head. I looked back and forth. I wasn't sure of my direction. I was disoriented. I stopped to rest for a few minutes, keeping my eye on that black hole.

Catching my breath, I started forward again, and pushed through the brush until I was close to the hole. I felt more than saw, a presence.

I stopped and studied the hole, peering and listening, ready to bolt. I was frightened but more curious, and more spooked than downright scared.

I watched the darkness within the stump for some moments. Then I thought I saw eyes, spots less black than the darkness that surrounded them. I blinked thinking my own eyes were playing tricks on me. I felt more than heard a low, deep growl. The eyes seemed to move toward me.

I straightened and tried to run, panicked now, but unable to move quickly because of the brambles.

I felt an asthma attack coming on. Breathless, now fighting for air, I reached for my inhaler. It wasn't in my pocket. I couldn't catch my breath.

I fell to the ground. The shadow of someone, or something, loomed over me. I lost consciousness.

Sometime later I woke.

My Brenda held me close.

We were on the deck behind the house.

"How did I get here?" I looked around. Sandy licked my face.

"I don't know, Sweetheart. I woke from my nap, and saw you lying on the deck. I rushed out to bring you my inhaler. What happened to you my Darling?"

"I don't know. All I remember is I began to lose it. I heard the bushes rustling. Then I was lifted up and the next I knew, I was here with you."

Alaska Steel

Steelhead, the great sea-run Rainbow Trout that runs in most of the Western coast of the United States and Canada, provides fine sport, especially in Southeastern Alaska where it is present in numbers especially in the coastal rivers of the Panhandle.

For each of five years I made an annual spring pilgrimage to Yakutat from which I floated for a few days among the bears, just emerging from their winter sleep, eagles, and the "Steelies," just beginning their own annual pilgrimage up the Situk River to spawn. Unlike salmon, which spawn and die, Steelhead live many years and return each year to spawn in their birth waters. The Situk Steelhead averaged six to ten pounds with some going more than twenty pounds.

They are fished for with flies and spinners, caught with salmon egg clusters preserved from the previous year's salmon fishing.

One year was special for me because I was taking my son on the float for his first shot at the big sea-run trout. Chris, in his early teens, had proven himself capable at handling most other kinds of Northern Pacific game fish including trout, halibut, and Chinook salmon. He was ready for the big time.

We arrived at the river near sundown. I was happy to see the river was moderately low and clear. We had rented a sixteen foot scow with which to drift with the gentle flow of the water, steering with oars and fishing the deep holes as we descended the river. The weather was partly cloudy. The temperature was mild. It was late April; too early for the mosquitoes that descended like a plague in June.

We decided to make camp for the night and start our float early the next morning. We pitched our pup tent on the river bank and rigged our spinning rods in hopes of catching a fresh steelhead for supper.

Not far upriver from camp, I spotted a likely riffle. I helped Chris rig up for fresh salmon eggs, and then tied on a yarn fly for myself.

I stepped slowly up to the edge of the water; taking care not to skyline myself or kick gravel and send unwanted vibrations to any fish lurking nearby. To my left and down the river, Chris was watching me and following my movements exactly.

Finally in position, I stood silently for a few moments, pretending to study the water. In fact I was glorying in God's good symphony of silence.

Selecting a spot above the riffle, I cast to it. Taking up slack as the sinker bounced along bottom, I followed the downward swing of my line with my rod tip. The tap-tap of the sinker against the stones along the bottom of the river sent an exciting message through my rod and up into my arm like electricity through a telegraph wire. It felt good and I was happy to be back on the river one more time.

The rhythm of the lead pencil sinker was a little too strong and the line jerked spasmodically. I knew I was carrying a little too much weight. Finishing the drift without a strike, I reeled in and clipped a little of the lead sinker. I adjusted the weight to allow a little more space above the fly.

I knew I should check Chris's weight, but wanted one more good drift first.

Casting a bit longer and closer to the far shore this time to adjust the drift pattern, I felt this was right.

The line moved down river, the sinker bouncing nicely now, and began to straighten at the end of the drift when I felt an indescribably subtle message that a fish had picked up the fly.

I waited an eternal moment and then snapped my wrist up, setting the hook—I hoped. I felt something so solid at the end of my line that I supposed I had hooked into a log, or a rock. I felt the tail of a fish work against my line and I knew I had hooked a steelhead—a big one by the feel of it.

In less time than it takes to tell about it that Steelie was airborne, incandescent array of silver and rainbow a dazzling sight.

Chris gave a "whoop!" and ran for the net. The big fish took to the air twice more, each time twisting and shaking in different directions, trying to rid itself of the hook. I saw that he was hooked solidly and prepared myself for the strong run I knew was inevitable. The fish ran straight toward me and I reeled madly, racing against its attempt to gain slack.

This was one wily Steelhead. It wheeled and headed for the far bank so fast I almost expected it to launch itself. Up and down river the fish fought against the breaking effect of the drag as I adjusted and readjusted it to compensate for the Steelie's erratic movements.

When it stopped in midstream to rest, I began to work him toward the near shore. Chris waited with the net at my side. "Looks like he's ready, Dad. Are you gonna bring him in right here?"

"Don't kid yourself, son. He's not near ready yet."

To confirm my words, the Steelhead made a short dash up river and punctuated it with a spectacular leap six or seven feet into the air. It made another shorter run downstream and another leap, this time a desperate awkward belly-flopping lunge. I knew the fish was tiring. Several runs made shorter each time as I increased the drag, culminated when it stopped in the shallows, rolled over, and submitted.

Chris netted the fish skillfully and we had it on shore. We had ourselves a ten pound buck—supper and breakfast as well.

This was the start of my most memorable fishing adventure. Wrapped snug and dry in my sleeping bag, later that same night, belly filled with fresh Steelhead cooked over and open fire, I thought about past trips and, as I drifted into sleep, anticipating the sheer beauty of the country bursting into wakefulness after the long Alaskan winter. I dreamed about formations of northbound geese and heard their excited calling accentuated by the slap of a beaver's tail, warning of my presence. I was pleased to be sharing this experience with my only son. The thrill of seeing it all afresh through his eyes presented a thrilling prospect.

Nothing ever happens in a small way in Alaska. I reckon that's why they call it "The Great Land."

Even a peaceful float down a meandering stream can quickly turn into a major adventure. Keep in mind that the landlord of any particular parcel of spectacular scenery may be a very large animal that may object to your presence on its turf.

I usually carry six votes for peaceful coexistence strapped to my hip just in case negotiations break down, but it's sometimes a little difficult to convince a startled, charging 800 pound Alaskan Brown Bear to stop and count the ballots. In my book the bear is boss. He can have anything he wants and I don't even think of asking Smith and Wesson to intervene unless what the bear wants is me. Most of the time the bears mind their own business and I mind mine.

The days were generally sunny and warm. The fishing was fantastic. Several runs of Steelhead had entered the river and were making their way to the spawning grounds at the head of the Situk. I had several days of catch and release adventures with the big sea run trout. Toward mealtimes I'd pick a smaller fish to cook for lunch or dinner.

The one sour note to this otherwise Valhalla-like fishing trip was Chris's persistent failure to land a fish. He'd hooked plenty of them and handled himself well, but each time the steelhead managed to outwit him. The boy was frustrated, his earlier exuberance over helping me land fish time and again, faded behind a wall of tight lipped silence.

Early on the fourth day I beached the boat on a sand bar above a likely looking slick running deep against and under the far bank, some twenty yards away. Most often Chris stayed pretty close by me, but this time he said, "Dad, I spotted a nice pool further down near that bend." He pointed downstream. "I'm gonna walk down there."

"Sure, Son. Just keep me in sight, okay?"

Chris nodded and started downstream.

My attention was diverted a moment later when I hung a large Steelie and was about to call for help with the net when the big rainbow spit the hook at me and headed for wherever fish go to say prayers of thanks for deliverance.

I was recovering my line when I heard Chris holler, "Fish on!"

I looked toward him just as a big fish cleared the water.

"Hang with him, Son! I'm coming!" I ran for the net. Then I changed my mind and slowed to a walk. I felt this was his fish and just maybe he could handle it better without my coaching. I picked up the net and ambled toward the scene of battle, enjoying the look of concentration on my son's face, remembering my own first Steelhead.

I approached the boy, fighting the urge to interfere with his personal struggle. I sat on a rock and chewed on a hunk of beef jerky as I watched the action.

"He's a big one, isn't he Dad!" Chris called over his shoulder when he realized I was with him. "You think we can keep him for supper?"

"I think you better land him before we warm up the skillet. Right now he appears to have ideas of his own."

As I uttered this last, the fish made a rod-cracking run upriver. I bit my tongue. My statement had made Chris nervous. The landing of this Steelhead was too important to him. His neck muscles grew taught. He was determined not to lose this fish.

I saw the line grow slack and I heard the boy moan, "Oh no!"

The air grew heavy with the deflation of his resolve. I stepped up beside Chris, desperately trying to think of words to make it right when the big Steelhead cleared the water just to our front and splashed, throwing water in our faces before it made another and final dash for freedom.

Chris smiled in a grim sort of way as he realized the fish was still hooked. The complaining "buzz" of his reel as it grudgingly gave up line was music to my ears. I knew Chris was going to win this one—and he did. Ten minutes later he had his first Steelhead netted, weighed, and held up for a private photo-op.

"How about that, Dad?" He said this with pride and sparkling eyes.

"I think we should release this big guy in honor of your first victory. He's too big to eat."

Chris thought for a moment before he walked to the edge of the river and gently place the fish back into the water. I was proud of Chris as I watched him walk the trout up and down the river, forcing water through his gills until; at last, the fish waved its tail and swam into deeper water.

"Dad, I'm glad we let this fish go. That way I can always think of him as mine."

I fought tears.

"We better get busy and catch another for supper tonight." I said.

That battle broke the ice for Chris. In the two days remaining of the float he caught and released as many Steelhead as I did. We took turns netting fish for each other. But I knew for sure he'd joined the ranks of inveterate steelheaders when, on the last day of our float, he'd lost a really nice trophy Steelhead after hooking it in an impossibly brush-cluttered pool. After five or more minutes of breathtaking aerobatics the fish wrapped the line around a submerged branch and that was that.

"That's okay, Dad. I knew I'd never get him out of there, but the fight was worth it."

This winter when the ice comes back we'll relax in front of a fire in the fireplace and catch those ol' iron heads again in our mind's eyes. We'll watch eagles, run from angry moose, and plan next year's float, not as coach and neophyte, but as equal partners in the sport of Steelheading.

DREAM OF FLIGHT

I dreamed I died and went to Heaven last night
As I entered I was greeted by an angel in white
Greetings said a voice
This day you'll be given a choice
Twixt passing your time
On subjects sublime
Or returning to earth
For a second birth
I asked for time to ponder if I'd like to stay
And if I went what creature I'd choose today
I do think said I It's a bird that I'd be
Not a hawk nor an eagle but a gull, you see
Why a gull you chose
I cannot suppose
Yet a gull it shall be
Said the angel to me
In sudden darkness I felt myself falling
I spread my arms, screaming and calling
Help . . . Screeeee . . . Scree . . . cried I
I am flying, O how glorious I can fly
Plummeting sliding
Swooping gliding
Communion with wind
No fault to rescind
I reveled in freedom from earth with glee
When suddenly appeared a hawk next to me
You think said the hawk you are a winner
I tell you tonight you'll serve as my dinner

Spinning and whirling
Falling and twirling
Earth coming fast
My death at the last
I awoke with a start my heart beating fast
By my bed I lay sprawled, blankets offcast
Shaking head looking about giving a squawk
Close by lay a feather from a red tailed hawk.

Walkers

A long day's work of unpacking boxes and moving furniture was over at the Donovan's new home. John and his wife Enola were readying for bed after a cold but relaxing supper of wine and cheese. Now they snuggled under the covers for some pillow talk.

"Well, what's on the schedule for tomorrow, 'Nola?"

"We're almost done. Those boxes in the kitchen are all that's left. They contain mostly dishes and kitchen stuff."

"Great! We'll get on 'em first thing tomorrow. Be done by noon."

"Oh, no," Enola said. "Not 'we,' Paleface. You know my rules for my kitchen. You do something else; go for a walk with that nice man next door. I'll take care of the kitchen. I'll make your favorite, spaghetti and meatballs for supper."

"Okay, Darlin,' whatever you say. But, golly gee whiz, I was sure looking forward to spending the day unpacking boxes."

"You take the morning off. Accept that fellow's invitation to show you around the neighborhood. What was his name?"

"Mitch. Mitch . . . Sorenson. A good Swede, I betcha."

"Go, take a walk with Mitch. Meet the neighbors. Tell them we love them, but stay away unless invited."

"Oh, you're a mean Bitch, Enola Donovan."

"You know I can be, John Donovan. We moved down from Seattle to these woods to get away from the crowds. I'm making a stand for privacy, you hear me?"

John reached for the lamp switch. He turned off the lamp, then took Enola in his arms and gave her a long, deep kiss.

She said lovingly, but finally, "Not tonight Johnnie. You may have the morning off but I have to work."

He sighed and rolled over on his back. The room was enveloped by their silence. "There's a moon tonight. I'm going to open the drapes. Maybe a little moonlight will change your mind."

"I'm going to sleep now."

John pulled the drapes open and cracked both windows. The night air, combined with the pale glow from the moon, shining through the firs, aroused him. He marched proudly back to bed, shaft at attention, waving from side to side.

Enola felt the urgent prodding against her hip.

"What was it Mitch had to say about the neighborhood walkers?"

John felt his erection beginning to falter. Then it wilted. The melody for the bugle call, *Taps*, ran momentarily through his mind and was as quickly forgotten.

"Mitch told me a few of the neighbors, mostly men, take daily walks around the neighborhood. He invited me to join them. 'Bring the missus too, if it pleases you,' he said, but he made it plain that it was a men's group.

"Did you notice how he looked when he smiled?"

"No. How did he look?"

"His lips curled back in a funny sorta doggie way. His canine teeth were prominent and longer than the usual. He reminded me of a golden retriever presenting a bird. If he'd had a tail, it would have been wagging . . . ."

Her heavy breathing told him Enola had fallen asleep.

He finished his narrative. "Anyway, he asked me to go on a walk with him tomorrow and I guess I'm going . . ." He slept.

Sometime after midnight, John was awakened by Enola's insistent shaking his shoulder.

"Wake up, Johnnie, wake up!"

"Wuh!"

John sat upright. He was immediately alert and on guard. His time in the Army had imbued him with that.

"Do you hear that? What, in God's name is that noise?"

They were both silent for a few moments. The moon shone full into their window. By its light, John could see that Enola was frightened. Her eyes reflected the moonlight.

Then he heard it. A drawn-out high pitched wail was answered by a series of yips. The sounds of barking added dimension. Enola clutched at him, trembling. A long, low, drawn out howl was followed by silence.

"John, Johnnie, what is that?"

John held her close. He wanted to laugh, but her obvious fear prevented that. He stroked her hair and calmed her down.

"That, 'Nola is a pack of coyotes. They're obviously on the hunt. Listen to them sing. They're making music just for us."

"Yeah, they're beautiful. Close the window and pull the drapes, please."

"Of course, Sweetheart. Whatever you say. Don't be afraid."

He got up and, after closing the window and drawing the drapes, returned to bed and wrapped her protectively in his arms. They fell asleep together,.

Arising early, they showered together, as was their custom, dressed and sat silently at the kitchen table enjoying their first cup of coffee. There was no mention of the previous night's events. Their thoughts were interrupted by the sound of a gong.

"What the hell is that?" John said.

"That, you dummy, is the doorbell!"

Enola grabbed both John's ears and shook. Both of them laughed as they hugged and kissed.

"Do I have to answer it?"

"Of course you do, you recalcitrant recidivist, it's probably Mitch, wanting you to go on a walkabout." She feigned an Aussie accent.

Standing at attention, he said, in his best British brogue, "Well, harrumph, if I must, I must."

He saluted with palm facing outward, stooped to give her a peck on the cheek, marched to the door and opened it.

"Howdy neighbor," Mitch smiled through his odd protruding canines. "I was wondering if you were going to take me up on my invitation for a guided tour of the neighborhood."

John looked back over his shoulder at Enola. She shrugged and blew him a kiss.

He turned back to Mitch, smiled and said, "Sure thing, Mitch. I've got my hiking shoes on and I'm rarin' to go."

As John stepped out and shut the door, Mitch said, "I thought we'd take a walk down to the beach. The trail starts just there."

He pointed toward a sign that John hadn't noticed before.

"The trail leads about a quarter of a mile down to Puget Sound where there's a dock and a boat ramp. After that we can walk around up here and meet some of the neighbors."

"Lead on, Mitch."

The trail was wide and well-traveled. John wasn't paying much attention to Mitch's travel-guide patter. His mind wandered as he enjoyed the walk. Every so often, Mitch would step off the trail to urinate against a tree.

"Sorry about that. Seems I have a bit of a prostate problem."

Under way once more, John said, "It's really beautiful here. I wouldn't be surprised if some of these massive old firs weren't a part of the primeval forest."

"Oh sure, you betcha. Think it's beautiful now; you oughta see it at night. Some of the walkers get together whenever the moon is full and stroll down to the beach by moonlight. We'll probably do that in a day or so. Maybe you'd like to join us."

"Sure. Ever bothered by the coyotes?"

Mitch looked at him sharply. "Coyotes? Oh, you mean the local pack that lives in this area. You probably heard them last night. Naw, they don't bother us. In fact they probably do us a favor by keeping our women inside. Men's night out don't you know?"

Both men chuckled as they broke out of the woods onto the beach.

The next evening, Enola and John were enjoying beer and pizza on the patio. The sun had gone down several hours earlier, but the air was warm. It was too early in the year for flying bugs. As he reached for a second slice of pizza, being sure to avoid that portion that was covered with jalapeno peppers, Enola's favorite topping, she said, "Are you really going traipsing down to the beach tonight with that bunch of overgrown boy scouts? What about the coyotes?"

"Sure, why not. Besides, those coyotes are there just to make sure it's a stag event. We may even do something racy like peeing in the woods. All boy scouts do that."

They laughed as together they tried to imagine a circle of old men urinating around a tree all at the same time.

"Just the same, I'm a little worried. You be sure to take a flashlight and your cell phone."

"Aw Mommy, we don't need no steenking flashlights," John said in his best Mexican-bandit- from-Treasure-of-Sierra-Madre-accent. "But I will take my phone, just to keep you happy. I'll call you if I need help fighting off hungry coyotes."

Just then the door-bell rang. John rose and stooped to give Enola a resounding kiss. "That's them. Don't worry, my Sweetheart, you don't get rid of me that easily. I'll try to be quiet when I come in, so as not to wake you."

As he moved toward the door, he called back, "I love you, my Darling."

She blew him a kiss in response.

John counted six neighbors gathered on his front porch. He'd met all of them during his tour with Mitch. Now they fidgeted as if anxious to be abroad. There was an atmosphere of expectation. John smiled inwardly. *Maybe there'll be fireworks.*

As a group they started toward the trail head. No one spoke. The moon was just rising over the treetops. John was

223

surprised at how little noise the others made. His own footsteps sounded heavily in his ears.

It was dark among the trees. He could make out the forms of only the two men ahead of him as they were silhouetted against the skyline. The others followed. The men moved in and out of the shadows formed by the trees under a full moon. The only sound other than John's footfalls was the intermittent chirping of tree frogs. The group stopped frequently as one or another of them urinated against a tree. John thought this strange in a group with only two who were obviously older than sixty.

Standing waiting on the trail, he suddenly realized he could see no one. The men had vanished. Then, as the clouds parted, and the moon shone brightly once more, John discovered himself surrounded by coyotes—No, *they aren't coyotes. They're dogs!* He was encircled by six dogs of varying breeds, but recognizable, individually as his walking companions.

One of the dogs raised his muzzle to the moon and gave a blood-curdling howl. Immediately the others joined in at varying pitches. Two of them yipped excitedly.

As one they pounced on John, biting and scratching. He fought to get free, but was borne to the ground. With all his strength he tried without success to regain his footing. The dogs were all over him. He reached a blackberry patch and struggled to hide himself among the thorns. The last he remembered was the pain of the thorns as he pulled the branches over him.

He awakened with a start. He was in his own bed. Enola snored lightly beside him. The drapes were pulled and it was dark. The hands on the luminous face of the clock read 0530.

Have I been dreaming? He rose, went to the bathroom and flicked the light switch on. He looked at his reflection in the floor-length mirror. He saw his arms and face were covered by dried blood and scratches. A blackberry thorn was buried deep in his right palm. He brought his palm up to his mouth, and using his teeth worked it out of the flesh. He chewed the thorn thoughtfully for a moment or two, and then spit it into the toilet. Here and there on his body he spotted bite marks. Examining himself more closely, he saw that none of the wounds were deep enough to be threatening.

He turned the shower full on. Then, shucking his underpants, John stepped under the flow of water. *Ah, that feels wonderful. I'll just wash off all the dried blood before 'Nola wakes.*

As if the thought of her was enough to invoke her presence, he heard her stirring in the next room. She entered the bathroom, dropped her night gown to the floor, and joined John in the shower.

The scent of her was strong in his nostrils. *What is that she is wearing? I'll have to get her to use it more often.*

Enola stepped close to John and kissed him deeply. Holding him closely she focused on his eyes. Then she stepped back, still holding his arms, and inspected his body up and down. "What on earth happened to you? You're covered with cuts and scratches."

"Had an argument with some blackberry bushes."

"Looks like the blackberries won. Turn around and let me do your back."

John turned his back to her and she began to scrub him all over.

He closed his eyes enjoying her ministrations.

"What is that perfume you're wearing? It's very . . . arousing."

"What? I'm not wearing anything."

"I'll say,"

He turned again to face her. She felt more than saw that he had a full erection.

"Oh my, Is that all for me?"

He said nothing, but turned her so that her back was facing him. He held her very close.

"Oooh, kinky!"

They stood making love this way. John bent frequently and nipped the back of her neck.

"Ow! You're hurting me. When did you get your teeth filed? Take it easy, Sweetheart."

At last, when both of them were sated and breathless, turning off the water, they dried each other with soft Turkish towels.

"Oh girl, I feel fantastic. Let's have some coffee."

John entered the kitchen after dressing, just as the coffee was finishing perking.

"Is that a new brand of coffee you're using 'Nola? It smells marvelous.'

"Nope. Same old stuff."

They sat together in the morning sunshine, each lost in thought as they enjoyed the hot, black coffee.

"Oh baby, I feel like I could lick the world. I think I'll take a walk down to the beach."

"I'll go with you," she said.

They started out down the path toward the beach. She felt marvelous. The wind coming up from the beach was invigorating. She smelled the flora and heard the fauna. She realized he wasn't with her. She turned in time to see him leave the trail and begin urinating against a tree.

She smiled.

THE FALCON AND THE BULLFROG

Kids these days get their thrills vicariously by electronic or other unnatural means. They've forgotten how to jump rope. They have forgotten how to make adventure happen. When I was a kid we used our imaginations to invent our worlds. We went fishing or hunting frogs and arrow heads. We built rafts and tree houses. We didn't depend on our parents to make our adventure for us. They were too busy eking out a living for the family.

I try to teach my eleven year old grandson how to make his own adventures and not wait around for some grownup to make them happen. A few weeks ago he was spending a few days with his grandma and me at our cottage near Joemma Beach. When he wasn't texting his friends, or playing a game on his Ipod, he was playing couch potato, watching TV.

"Hey, Matt, you wanna go for a bike ride with me?"

"Naw. Too hot."

"How about we feed the fish?" I keep a small pond with a few Koi and goldfish in the back yard.

"Well. . . Okay. Sure."

A couple of handfuls of fish feed thrown to them and he was ready to go back to the couch and Sponge Bob.

I prepared a little surprise for his next visit. Rick Roland, the owner of the Horseshoe Lake Golf Course, near the north end of the Key Peninsula is a friend of mine. I ran into him the other day.

"Say Rick, how about letting me hunt bullfrogs in your water hazards one night next week?"

"Sure. What are you planning to do with the frogs?"

"Eat them, of course. Haven't you ever eaten frog's legs?"

"No, I never have. How do you fix them?"

"I roll the legs in a mixture of corn meal and corn starch and sauté them in butter and white wine. You ought to see those suckers hop around in the frying pan."

"What do they taste like?"

"Kinda like chicken but better because the meat is more muscular. Gives 'em texture"

"Well, knock yourself out."

"Great. Thanks, Rick. I'll bring my grandson out some night next week. Probably Thursday."

"Just give me a call and I'll open the gate for you."

When I told Brenda about my plan, she thought it was a great idea. I asked her not to mention anything about it to Matt. I wanted to surprise him and see if I could get him to think it was his idea to go frogging.

On Wednesday, his first day with us, we had some of Brenda's wonderful southern fried chicken for supper.

"How do you like that chicken, Matt?"

"Great," he said between bites." He loved his grandma's cooking. He believed she was "the best cook in the whole world."

"You know your grandma always says I married her for her Georgia fried chicken." I winked at Brenda across the table.

"Well it's true," she said.

"About the only thing that tastes as good as your fried chicken is a good mess of crawdads or frog legs. We can't get any crawfish around here but there are some awesome bullfrogs in the water holes up at the golf course."

"Bullfrogs? Are they really good eatin,' Grandpa?"

He had taken the bait.

"You bet your life. Of course we only eat the legs."

"Do you think we could catch some?"

He was hooked.

"Maybe. Gotta go after dark though. It's the only time we can get close to them. Let's go out to the garage and see if I got the right gear."

As we walked to the garage, I saw the kind of excitement in Matt's eyes that I was looking for.

"Okay. First we need a long fishing rod." I keep my twenty or so rods in the rafters in the roof of the garage. "This salmon rig oughta do the job. Now we need a treble hook." I dug one out of my tackle box and tied it onto the nylon line wound onto the spool of my old Penn fishing reel.

"What'll we use for bait, Grandpa?"

"Well let's see now," I looked around on my messy work bench. I spotted an old orange work towel. "Ah, this ought to do the job." I tore a strip off one corner and stuck it on the hook. "Don't ask me why, but if we dangle this bit of colored cloth in front of ol' bullfrog's nose, he'll jump at it. Must think it's a bug. Anyway it worked in the East when I was your age. Oughta work the same here. I got a burlap bag we can put the frogs in. Now all we need's a flashlight and we'll be set. You are now the official flashlight holder. You don't mind getting a little wet do you?"

'No, Grandpa." He was really for it now.

We left the house just before dark and drove the ten miles up to the golf course. I picked the water hole most likely to give up big bullfrogs.

We stood on the darkening shore and worked the light back and forth over the surface of the water. We walked among the cattails.

"There's one!" Matt sang out. We saw the eyes of the frog reflected in the flashlight beam. I handed him the light and said, "Hold it on him as steady as you can."

I waded out into the warm, August pond water. I felt like a kid again, hunting bullfrogs in the mill pond back in Massachusetts, during the war. I always think of bullfrogs as male. I know there must be male and female bullfrogs, but thinking about female bullfrogs seems like such an oxymoron. About the only way to tell one sex from the other is open them up. If there's eggs, it's a female. Duh.

I waded as close to the frog as I dared and swung the lure out in front of his face. Once . . . twice . . . . No reaction from the frog. I was starting to worry. On the third try, the frog jumped for the lure and was snagged by the hook. I swung it to shore, grabbed it, and freed it from the hook.

"Aw, this one's too small, but we'll put it in the bag and set it free in my fish pond at home. Now let's find a bigger one."

We walked back and forth along the shore.

"There's one Grandpa, and he's humongous."

Matt shined his light in the bulrushes close to shore. I repeated the dance of the rag and soon hooked the frog. As I swung him into the air, I could tell he weighed at least two pounds. He came loose before he hit the ground.

Like an Airedale, Matt was on him.

"Good boy! Great save. Put him in the sack. He's food for sure. Look at the size of those legs!"

We fished for a couple of more hours. We were wet and muddy and starting to grow tired. We'd only managed to land three bullfrogs.

"Oh, man I'm gettin' tired. I believe we better quit. We don't have enough legs to eat. I suppose we ought to let them go. None of them are really injured at all."

I could see that Matt was tired and disappointed as well.

"Wait. I got an idea. Why don't we put all three of them in my fish pond? I'll bet they'd like it. Better a big frog in a small pond than a small frog in a big pond, eh?"

Missing the point of my attempt at pond-side humor, with a sleepy smile Matt agreed. We packed our gear and started for home.

We opened the bag and spilled the frogs into my fish pond. The frogs appeared happy to be freed from the burlap. One, from the sound of his B-a-a-r-o-o-mph, the largest of the trio, seemed to be making himself right at home.

My mission was accomplished. Matt had learned that the best adventures come not from an electronic device, but from the reality of experience.

Brenda said, "I heard that frog sounding off. If that keeps up, I'm going to be an unhappy camper."

Several days went by and the frogs settled in nicely with my goldfish. I hadn't had trouble with raccoons since I'd steepened the banks a couple of years ago and deepened it considerably. It was about ten feet across and four feet deep. Owl and osprey visited occasionally, but they offered little threat beyond the occasional loss of a fish.

One afternoon, Brenda and I were relaxing on the front porch watching the comings and goings of a pair of juncos nesting in the front yard. They were busy feeding chicks. Without warning, so fast I nearly missed it; a raptor swooped down and, snatched one of the juncos in midflight.

"What was that?" Brenda asked. "Was that a crow? He snatched one of my birds."

"No. Too fast for a crow. It was a raptor of some kind. We'll have to watch the nest closely now. The babies may require help to survive." We'd been through this scenario of orphaned chicks before.

A few days later, I sat at my computer, working on a new book. I was searching for inspiration and sat watching the big guy bullfrog sitting in the grass by our fish pond, waiting for bugs. A dozen or so small birds, including a pair of goldfinches, clustered near the bird feeder, jockeying for position. They took turns bathing in the waterfall.

I sat dreamily watching this panorama. The bullfrog suddenly took a great hop for the center of the pond. The birds scattered. Midway through his hop he collided with a large bird or the bird collided with the frog. I barely comprehended what had happened when the bird disappeared and the frog dropped into the pond.

I wasn't certain I'd seen correctly. *Has someone thrown a rock and hit my frog?* I ran outside. The frog seemed a bit stunned but otherwise unhurt. I looked around for the bird and found nothing beyond a few feathers. Some movement caught my eye and I looked at the split rail fence that surrounds our front yard. There, on a post stood a peregrine falcon shaking its head and preening its feathers. Apparently all two pounds of my bullfrog, startled by the sudden appearance of the raptor and trying to flee to the safety of the pond, had intercepted the falcon's diving attempt to capture one of the little birds.

The falcon flew away, not to return. *Bullfrogs—1, raptors—0,* I thought as I returned to my work, inspired now to write a story. It began like this—"I used to think we had to make our adventures. It seems I was wrong. Sometimes they come to us, unbidden."

THE CLOSET OF MY YESTERDAYS

I wander down the hall
Open a door
And enter the closet of my yesterdays.

Inside are boxes stacked on boxes
Inside each box is a memory
Reaching for one, I open it

Suddenly I'm looking into your eyes
On a summer's day
When we were young
The first time we met

The Time Machine

"Grandpa, what was it like when you were as old as me?"

My Grandson, Matt, was just turned ten. He had been caught texting when he was supposed to be doing something else. His punishment was to spend some time with his grandparents.

"Well, Matt, things were a lot different then. It's kind of hard to explain. Maybe I can show you. Step into my time machine." I put my hand on Matt's shoulder and guided him into my office. Chloe my old Golden Retriever followed. As usual it was messy, scraps of unfinished manuscript strewn about. There was lots of desk space, none of it uncovered.

"This isn't a time machine," my grandson scolded.

"Oh yes it is, young man. From here I can go anywhere, anytime, see anything, do anything I want."

Matt didn't say anything. He cocked his head and looked at me with unbelieving eyes.

We sat down in the two comfortable office chairs I keep there; one for working, one for dreaming. I offered Matt my dreaming chair. Chloe plopped down between the boy and me. Behind us the wall was lined with books. There were cases filled with mementos against the other walls. Hanging all around, were my many "brag rags" from glory days in service of Her Majesty of the United States, Queen Liberty. I wasn't sure I could claim that my exploits were for Democracy or for the United States. Those words had fallen into disrepute of late. Lots of words I had held in respect were gone to hell. I had no way of knowing what the boy held dear.

"Matt, I want you to empty your pockets."

He reached into his right pocket and took out a cell-phone and some coins. In his left pocket he removed a plastic box that he identified as a Game Boy. I didn't ask him what it was used for. "Grandpa, you're foolin' me again. This isn't a time machine."

"Well, we'll see about that. Tell me what great adventure you've experienced lately. Close your eyes and think." Matt closed his eyes and leaned back in the leather chair. "Relax . . . Just relax . . . I want you to put yourself back where you were when you were experiencing your most thrilling adventure in the last year."

After a few moments of silence I said, "Where are you Matt?"

"I'm remembering being at Wild Waves."

"Good. Now I want you to place yourself more into the adventure. Don't just remember being at Wild Waves, be there."

Matt opened his eyes. I placed my hand in front of his face and said, "Keep your eyes closed and think about how it was in the water. Now be at wild waves. Feel how it was coming down the slide. Feel how it felt when the waves began to pound gently on your body."

We were both silent for a few moments. I was beginning to think Matt had gone to sleep.

"Matt. What's happening?"

Matt opened his eyes wide. He looked at me and smiled.

"Oh, Grandpa, I really was at wild waves. I see what you mean. This really is a time machine."

"You asked me what it was like when I was your age. Now I can tell you and you will understand. I had a time machine called my imagination. With it I could go anywhere, do

237

anything, and be anybody. You can do the same. You don't need my time machine. You have your own, right here," I tapped the side of his head with my finger.

He was quiet for a moment. Then he looked at me and spoke very seriously, "Grandpa, when I grow up I want to be just like you."

"Well, my boy, you flatter me, but when you grow up I want you to be just like you."